Educating for Cosmopolitanism

Also by Mark Bracher

LITERATURE AND SOCIAL JUSTICE: Protest Novels, Cognitive Politics, and Schema Criticism (*2013*)

SOCIAL SYMPTOMS OF IDENTITY NEEDS: Why We Have Failed to Solve Our Social Problems, and What to Do About It (*2009*)

RADICAL PEDAGOGY: Identity, Generativity, and Social Transformation (*2006*)

THE WRITING CURE: Psychoanalysis, Composition, and the Aims of Education (*1999*)

LACAN, DISCOURSE, AND SOCIAL CHANGE: A Psychoanalytic Cultural Criticism (*1993*)

BEING FORM'D: Thinking through Blake's Milton (*1985*)

palgrave▸pivot

Educating for Cosmopolitanism: Lessons from Cognitive Science and Literature

Mark Bracher
Professor, Department of English, Kent State University, USA

DOI: 10.1057/9781137390202

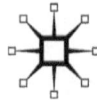

EDUCATING FOR COSMOPOLITANISM
Copyright © Mark Bracher, 2013.

All rights reserved.

First published in 2013 by
PALGRAVE MACMILLAN®
in the United States—a division of St. Martin's Press LLC,
175 Fifth Avenue, New York, NY 10010.

Where this book is distributed in the UK, Europe and the rest of the world, this is by Palgrave Macmillan, a division of Macmillan Publishers Limited, registered in England, company number 785998, of Houndmills, Basingstoke, Hampshire RG21 6XS.

Palgrave Macmillan is the global academic imprint of the above companies and has companies and representatives throughout the world.

Palgrave® and Macmillan® are registered trademarks in the United States, the United Kingdom, Europe and other countries.

ISBN: 978-1-137-39022-6 EPUB
ISBN: 978-1-137-39020-2 PDF
ISBN: 978-1-137-39226-8 Hardback

Library of Congress Cataloging-in-Publication Data is available from the Library of Congress.

A catalogue record of the book is available from the British Library.

First edition: 2013

www.palgrave.com/pivot

DOI: 10.1057/9781137390202

*For my daughters,
Elizabeth Bracher and Victoria Bracher,
and their generation's pursuit of global justice*

Contents

Acknowledgments ... vii

1 What Is Cosmopolitanism, and How Can Education Promote It? ... 1

2 How Cognitive Science Can Help Us Educate for Cosmopolitanism ... 10

3 Correcting Ethnocentric Prototypes of Self and Other with Achebe's *Things Fall Apart* ... 25

4 Developing Metacognition of Ethnocentrism with Lessing's "The Old Chief Mshlanga" and Voltaire's *Candide* ... 51

5 Correcting Faulty General Person-Schemas with *Things Fall Apart*, "The Old Chief Mshlanga," and *Candide* ... 94

6 Developing Cosmopolitan Action Scripts with Camus's "The Guest" and Coetzee's *Disgrace* ... 106

Works Cited ... 129

Index ... 137

Acknowledgments

I thank Masood Raja for jump-starting this stalled project by inviting me to contribute a chapter to his collection *Critical Pedagogy and Global Literature: Worldly Teaching* (Palgrave Macmillan, 2013) and to Palgrave Macmillan for permission to reprint a slightly revised version of that chapter as the first two chapters here. Thanks also to Kent State University's Research Council and Office of Research and Sponsored Programs for providing me with a research leave that enabled me to complete this book in a timely manner. My daughters, Elizabeth Bracher and Victoria Bracher, with their commitment to education and global justice, have helped keep my cosmopolitan hope alive in the face of daunting obstacles to its realization. And my partner and colleague Tammy Clewell, in addition to recommending Coetzee's *Disgrace* and stimulating my thinking on a daily basis with her intelligence, grace, and wit, has gifted me love and joy that make work seem like play.

palgrave▸pivot

www.palgrave.com/pivot

1
What Is Cosmopolitanism, and How Can Education Promote It?

Abstract: *What are the specific learning objectives that will most effectively promote cosmopolitanism, defined as the commitment to reduce suffering throughout the world and promote global justice? This chapter argues that the formation of cosmopolitans requires developing the cognitive capabilities of recognizing, when the facts warrant, the need of distant peoples, understanding how they are not (or at least not primarily) responsible for their need, and apprehending their sameness or intimate connectedness with oneself. When such judgments are made, the result is compassion for the other, which in turn leads to assistance for the other. Developing these cognitive capabilities involves correcting or replacing certain faulty information-processing structures that prevent us from recognizing these truths.*

Mark Bracher. *Educating for Cosmopolitanism: Lessons from Cognitive Science and Literature.* New York: Palgrave Macmillan, 2013. DOI: 10.1057/9781137390202.

In her presidential address to the Modern Language Association several years ago, Domna Stanton proposed "cosmopolitanism as an educational ideal" for literary study (629). She argued that although "we do not typically see ourselves as the heirs of cosmopolitanism,... what we, the teacher-scholars of the MLA, do in our many diverse ways is to exemplify and promote a cosmopolitan education" (629). Specifically,

> when we read "foreign" texts in the original or in translation, we advocate an encounter with people who are markedly different from and at the same time much like ourselves—a complex encounter made in a sympathetic effort to see the world as they see it and, as a consequence, to denaturalize our own views. Those pedagogical practices involve cosmopolitanism by implicitly rejecting parochial, chauvinistic beliefs in the exclusive value of our language, culture, nation or ethnos and by inherently embracing diversity as fundamental to the construction of the self in—and as—its relation to others. (629)

Stanton concluded her speech by calling for a concerted effort on the part of language and literature teacher-scholars to form our students into cosmopolitans: in "teaching the languages and the literatures of the world in the classroom," she declared, "*we must try to form citizens* not only *of* the world but also *for* the world" (638; first emphasis added; other emphases in original).

This is certainly a worthy aim, for "as a fundamental devotion to the interests of humanity as a whole" rather than to more limited groups (Robbins, "Introduction" 1; see also Nussbaum, "Patriotism" 4, 7; Malcomson 234; Anderson 274; Lu 264), cosmopolitanism entails "a desire to change the world" (Malcomson 234) so as "to diminish suffering regardless of colour, class, religion, sex and tribe" (Hollinger 230). As Derek Heater notes, cosmopolitanism is based on the ethical principle of "the equal worth of all human beings as world citizens" (Heater 9), and this principle, as Catherine Lu observes, "provides us with a morally compelling view of how our many worlds may meet, as they inevitably will, on terms of humanity, justice, and tolerance, which are the foundations of perpetual peace and friendship, rather than on terms of cruelty, inequity, and violence, the foundations of perpetual war and animosity" (Lu 265; see also Robbins, "Cosmopolitanism" 49, 51).[1]

What, then, beyond the general parameters noted by Stanton, are the specific learning objectives through which literary study can most effectively pursue the worthy aim of forming cosmopolitans? Contrary to the assumption of many of its proponents, cosmopolitan education must involve much more than the acquisition of knowledge about other peoples. As Heater states it, "Knowledge and understanding about developing countries, which is sometimes almost equated with education for world citizenship..., misses the very heart of the matter" (172). Cosmopolitan education, Heater argues, "should rightly be as much about... *acquiring appropriate attitudes and behaviour patterns* as about acquiring knowledge" (177; emphasis added). But what are the "appropriate attitudes and behaviour patterns" for cosmopolitans? Or, as James Donald puts the question, "What... would cosmopolitan... graduates *be* in the second decade of the 21st century? What could we reasonably expect such graduates to be able to *do*? And what knowledge and expertise would enable them to be what they need to be and to do what they need to do?" (296; emphasis in original).

It is thus necessary to begin by determining three things:

1 the specific behaviors that constitute cosmopolitanism (see Heater 177);
2 the capabilities and habits of mind and heart that enable and motivate these behaviors (see Donald 296; Skrbis et al. 127); and
3 the types of educational practices that foster these cosmopolitan capabilities and habits of mind and heart (see Stevenson 258).

As various discussants of cosmopolitanism have noted, none of these tasks has yet been accomplished (Skrbis 127–128; Vertovec and Cohen 21). Indeed, few proponents of cosmopolitanism explicitly identify the specific behaviors that cosmopolitanism entails, and many appear not even to have recognized that certain psychological changes, and hence also the activities or experiences that produce these changes, are prerequisites for the establishment of cosmopolitanism (see Stevenson 265). As Vertovec and Cohen have observed, "While the trend towards positively reappropriating notions of cosmopolitanism is to be welcomed for its socially and politically transformative potential, practically all the recent writings on the topic remain in the realm of rhetoric. There is little description or analysis of how contemporary cosmopolitan philosophies, political projects, outlooks or practices can be formed, instilled or bolstered. In short, there are few recipes for fostering cosmopolitanism" (21; see also Robbins, "Introduction" 3; Beck 29).

The first question, concerning the types of behavior that constitute cosmopolitanism, is fairly easy to answer: cosmopolitanism entails helping others who are in need, no matter who or where they are. Although commentators disagree concerning how much one should be expected to sacrifice in order to meet these obligations, there is considerable consensus concerning the existence of an obligation to help others in need, including distant strangers (see Appiah 143–174). As Appiah puts it, for cosmopolitans "every human being has obligations to every other" (144). The most general helping behaviors include, as we have already noted in passing, "assist[ing] others in danger or distress" (Heater 185), "interven[ing] against active and passive injustice" (Lu 264), and "diminish[ing] suffering regardless of colour, class, religion, sex and tribe" (Hollinger 230). More specific behaviors include actions such as voting and activism in support of human rights and distributive justice—and whatever else may be needed to support their dignity and well-being—for all individuals everywhere (see Tan).

What are the psychological factors, then, that lead people to act in ways that provide help for others, including distant strangers, who are in need? Here the discussions to date are considerably less helpful, for the psychological traits most commonly ascribed to cosmopolitans are incapable by themselves of producing the helping behavior that constitutes the substance of cosmopolitanism. As Skrbis, Kendall, and Woodward observe, "commentators commonly suggest that in terms of 'disposition', cosmopolitanism should be understood principally as an attitude of 'openness' toward others [sic] cultures" (127; see also Donald 299). But as these authors go on to point out, "the notion of openness...is rather vague and diffuse. How is such openness manifested, and what are the sentiments that are embedded within the general attitudinal category of openness?" (Skrbis et al. 127). Their own suggestions, however—"that 'cultural openness' can be manifested in various ways, including...in both intellectual and aesthetic domains" and that "it must also involve emotional and moral/ethical commitments," including "an empathy for and interest in other cultures" (127–128)—do little to advance our understanding of this issue, and the authors rightly conclude that "more research needs to address the specific elements of a cosmopolitan disposition" (128).

Other commentators have suggested that the key psychological factor in cosmopolitanism is a "larger loyalty" (Rorty) or a sense of global citizenship. Heater, for example, argues that cosmopolitanism depends on "an understanding of the nature and significance of world citizenship to the point where it is not questioned, ignored or derided, but accepted as a normal feature of one's social life" (185). Heater believes that if "more people...think more deeply that they belong to a global community and...accept the moral implications of that membership..., this might lead...to a global community in which 'the obligation to assist others in danger or distress was a powerful imperative'" (185). This argument would appear to be supported by studies finding that the establishment of a common, superordinate identity for two groups enhances positive attitudes and cooperation between them. However, since *national* citizenship does not motivate people to aid all other individuals in their own nation, it is hard to see how a sense of *global* citizenship would motivate them to aid distant strangers around the world. Something more than just a common group membership is therefore necessary.

The most significant psychological factor of cosmopolitanism that has been identified is compassion for strangers. As Stanton and others have pointed out, Martha Nussbaum has advocated a form of cosmopolitan education centered on literary study that promotes such compassion in readers (Stanton 631–632; Donald 303–304; Heater 155; Vertovec and Cohen 21). In *Cultivating Humanity,* Nussbaum claims (following Marcus Aurelius) "that to become world citizens we must not simply amass knowledge; we must also cultivate in ourselves a capacity for sympathetic imagination that will enable us to comprehend the motives and choices of people different from ourselves, seeing them not as forbiddingly alien and other, but as sharing many problems and possibilities with us" (85). Literature, Nussbaum maintains, is particularly crucial for cosmopolitanism because it promotes "an expansion of sympathies that real life cannot cultivate sufficiently" (*Cultivating* 111). She concludes that "[i]f the literary imagination develops compassion, and if compassion is essential for civic responsibility, then we have good reason to teach works that promote the types of compassionate understanding that we want and need" (*Cultivating* 99).

As attractive as Nussbaum's claim is, however, it fails to offer evidence in support of the two key assumptions on which it is based: that "the literary imagination develops compassion" for real people (as opposed to fictional characters) and that "compassion is essential for civic responsibility." There is ample evidence to support the second proposition, that compassion for strangers leads people to assume responsibility for their welfare. There is ubiquitous anecdotal evidence that, as Robert Solomon observes, "one can hardly feel compassion without wanting to do something to change the world, to end the suffering" (244; see also Nussbaum, *Upheavals* 335). And there is also significant empirical evidence supporting this point. As the psychologist Bernard Weiner explains, empirical studies demonstrate that emotions are often the primary immediate causes of behavior: "affects are the more proximal and more important determinants of behavior than thoughts are.... The proximal or immediate causes of conduct are affective reactions. That is, feelings are determined by thoughts, and then the personal actions are based on those feelings rather than on the underlying cognitions" (174, 82). And since the emotion of compassion—which a leading emotion researcher has defined as "being moved to distress by another person's suffering, and wanting to help" (Lazarus and Lazarus 125)—"promotes help giving" (Weiner 82), compassion for all humans, no matter who or where they are, advances the central cosmopolitan goal of "justice without borders" (Tan) by promoting help-giving for all people. There is thus good evidence to support Nussbaum's claim that increasing people's capacity to experience compassion for others who are quite different from them is central to the formation of cosmopolitans.

What, then, of Nussbaum's other assumption, that "the literary imagination develops compassion"? In *Cultivating Humanity*, Nussbaum claims that reading certain types of literature "develops compassion" (99) and "broaden[s] sympathy" (93). But here, too, she offers no substantial evidence to support her claim. Instead, her argument relies upon an equivocation: the compassion that is developed and broadened refers both to the compassion readers feel for characters in a text and the compassion they feel for real people outside the text. Nussbaum appears to assume that by arousing sympathy for characters, literature also automatically heightens and broadens readers' sympathy for real people. But while it is obvious that literature often develops compassion for characters in the text and also broadens readers' sympathy by extending it to characters who are strange and different from readers, it is not at all evident that readers who have their sympathy for characters developed and broadened go on to experience greater compassion for real strangers outside the text. Indeed, there are clear cases of individuals feeling great compassion for suffering characters and yet remaining indifferent or even hostile to real people in need who are right in front of them. Rudolph Hess, for example, is said to have wept for characters in an opera being performed during the Holocaust by condemned Jewish prisoners toward whom he remained impassive, and William James relates the story of a wealthy woman weeping at the plight of characters in a play while her servants waited outside in freezing weather (see Solomon 233). In sum, as

Suzanne Keen has observed, there is little evidence to support the notion "that novel reading, by eliciting empathy [and through empathy, sympathy], encourages prosocial action and good world citizenship" ("Theory" 224): "The [presumed] set of links among novel reading, experiences of narrative empathy, and altruism has not yet been proven to exist" (Keen, *Empathy* viii). Indeed, Keen wonders "whether the expenditure of shared feeling on fictional characters might not waste what little attention we have for others on nonexistent entities" (*Empathy* xxv). Noting that "the empirical evidence for causal links between fiction reading and the development of empathy in readers does not yet exist," Keen concludes that "whether novels on their own can actually extend readers' empathic imagination and make prosocial action more likely remains uncertain" (*Empathy* 124, 116).

If experiencing sympathy for literary characters does not reliably lead to compassion—and thereby to help-giving—for strangers around the world, what, if anything, can literary study do to promote the compassion for real (as opposed to fictional) strangers that constitutes the core of cosmopolitanism? Nussbaum herself points to a more promising possibility in *Upheavals of Thought: The Intelligence of Emotions*, published several years after *Cultivating Humanity*. In this more recent book she recognizes that compassion is produced not only by empathy but also, and more fundamentally, by specific judgments, or appraisals, concerning people in need, and that therefore the most effective way to promote cosmopolitan compassion is to develop the capability and habit of making these compassion-producing appraisals for all people in need. Following Aristotle and contemporary cognitive appraisal theories of emotion, Nussbaum identifies three judgments that are collectively both necessary and sufficient to produce compassion:

1. that another person has a serious need or is experiencing significant suffering (*Upheavals* 306–311);
2. that the other is not responsible for this suffering or need (*Upheavals* 311–315); and
3. that the other's well-being overlaps significantly with one's own (*Upheavals* 315–321).

When people make these three judgments (explicitly or implicitly), they feel compassion, and when one or more of these judgments is absent, the compassion is either vitiated or absent entirely. Othering involves denying one or more of these three facts about other people. And cosmopolitan justice requires reaching each of these three conclusions, when the facts warrant.[2] Thus while empathy often serves as a path to compassion, it is in and of itself neither necessary nor always sufficient for the production of compassion (*Upheavals* 327–335). A series of studies done to test the relative importance of empathy and perceived oneness, or self-other overlap, with others in determining helping behavior found that "decisions to help were influenced by perceptions of oneness [with others] but not by levels of empathic concern" per se (Cialdini et al. 489). From these studies, the researchers concluded that "[e]mpathic concern is not the functional cause of helping but a concomitant of perceived oneness, which is the functional cause.... [I]t is because the self is [perceived to be] implicated in the other that the other's welfare is valued and promoted...; the primary role of empathic concern is to serve as an emotional signal of oneness" (Cialdini et al. 483, 491).

Empathy is also a means for perceiving the other's suffering. Indeed, the perception of the other's suffering is often a result of some form of empathy or mind reading, as research on mirror neurons indicates (see Iacoboni). Other studies have found that empathy is also a means to the perception of the other's situatedness, and thus a check on the tendency to blame victims for their own suffering, an example of what psychologists refer to as the "fundamental attribution error" (see Vescio et al.).

It is thus not empathy per se but rather the three cognitive appraisals that are both necessary and sufficient for producing compassion and helping. This means that even if literature does not increase readers' empathy for peoples around the world, it could still increase compassion for them—and thus promote cosmopolitan "justice without borders"—by increasing their compassion-producing appraisals of Others. And this fact suggests that an education that aims to form students into cosmopolitans needs to develop their ability and inclination to make these three compassion-producing appraisals whenever they are valid—that is, concerning needy strangers everywhere.

Nussbaum recognizes this fact. "If we are persuaded that appropriate compassion is an important ingredient of good citizenship," she states, "then we will want to give public support to procedures by which this ability is taught" (*Upheavals* 425). But while she acknowledges that this means cultivating the three appropriate judgments (*Upheavals* 425), when she tries to explain how to do this through literary study, she falls back on the arguments from *Cultivating Humanity* about engaging students in perspective taking and empathy, stating "that empathic imagining is an extremely valuable aid to the formation of appropriate judgments and responses" (*Upheavals* 432). But again, while it is true that empathy *can* be a path to compassion by leading to the three compassion-producing appraisals, it does not *necessarily* do so, as we have seen, and more importantly, as we have also noted, there is no clear evidence that empathy for characters necessarily leads to greater empathy for real people. For these reasons, we cannot expect empathic imagining regarding literary characters to be a reliable means of producing the three compassion-producing appraisals of real people.

We are thus left with the question of how the study of literature might promote the capacity and tendency to make the three compassion-producing judgments of real people when they are warranted by the facts. Studies in social cognition and cognitive therapy provide the resources for answering this question. This research has found that our perceptions and judgments of other people—and hence also our emotions and actions regarding them—are produced by cognitive structures that govern multiple information-processing activities, and that when these structures are faulty, they can be corrected by engaging subjects in certain cognitive activities that, as I will show, literary study is ideally positioned to engage readers in.

Notes

1 For other views on, and dimensions of, cosmopolitanism, see Brown and Held; Cheah; Held; and Turner.
2 This is precisely what Harriet Beecher Stowe helped white readers of *Uncle Tom's Cabin* do, demonstrating that, contrary to the dominant white racist assumptions (1) the slaves suffered just as much as white people when separated from loved ones, (2) the slaves did not bear primary responsibility for their suffering, or for their bad behavior, or even for their bad character, and (3) the slaves were fundamentally just like white people in terms of their capabilities and their vulnerabilities. These corrections in white readers' appraisals of slaves increased their compassion for slaves, which in turn increased their support for the abolitionist movement (see Bracher, "How").

2
How Cognitive Science Can Help Us Educate for Cosmopolitanism

Abstract: *The key to increasing the defining element of cosmopolitanism—helping distant others who are in need—is to increase people's recognition of their sameness and overlap with Others. Changing their habitual distorted—and sometimes dehumanizing—perception of Others, however, usually requires much more than evidence and logical argument. It requires replacing faulty cognitive schemas, which comprise not just faulty propositional beliefs about Others but also multiple non-propositional forms of faulty knowledge. Correcting faulty schemas can be accomplished by practices such as the encoding in memory of powerful corrective exemplars of the Other and developing metacognition of one's cognitive and emotional responses to the Other. Literature can initiate these schema-altering processes in readers, and teachers can enhance them through practices that are explained here.*

Mark Bracher. *Educating for Cosmopolitanism: Lessons from Cognitive Science and Literature.* New York: Palgrave Macmillan, 2013. DOI: 10.1057/9781137390202.

What we need to identify are the cognitive structures that prevent people from arriving at the three compassion-producing judgments about others when these judgments are warranted. That is, what cognitive structures are responsible for the perception that certain people are not suffering when in fact they are, for the judgment that certain people are solely responsible for their plight when in fact they are not, and for the conclusion that certain people's being does not overlap with one's own when in fact it does? Here, too, cognitive science provides answers. Research in social cognition (i.e., people's perception and judgment of others) indicates that certain faulty cognitive structures that control our social information processing are largely responsible for the three incorrect, compassion-inhibiting judgments about others. Studies also demonstrate that when these faulty structures are replaced by more adequate ones that produce more accurate and comprehensive perceptions and judgments of others, the result is greater compassion and assistance for the Other.

Cognitive schemas

The key cognitive structures that lead to the three mistaken judgments concerning the Other are cognitive schemas of particular groups of persons and of persons in general. Cognitive schemas are general knowledge structures that comprise multiple types and forms of knowledge concerning a particular category.[1] The basic types of knowledge include propositional knowledge (based in semantic memory), knowledge of particular instances and events (based in episodic memory), prototypes (generalizations or averages of these particular instances and events), and information-processing scripts (based in procedural memory). Any or all of these four types of knowledge can play a significant role in our perception, judgment, emotion, and action regarding other people, determining what we perceive about them, what we focus our *attention* on, what *inferences* and *suppositions* we make about them, what sort of information about them we *search for* when it is not present, what information about them is *encoded* in our memory (and how it is encoded), what we *recall* about them, what *emotions* we have in response to them, and what *actions* we take in regard to them, including what public policies we support.

Prototypes and dehumanization

When it comes to perceiving and judging Others—people who belong to an outgroup rather than to one of our ingroups—the type of knowledge that often plays the main role in guiding our assessment of them is the stereotype, which is a prototype that is automatically (and usually unconsciously) activated whenever we process information about a particular category of person.[2] Thus historically and still today, when many Westerners consider Africans, their perception, judgment, emotion, and action are governed by their prototype (stereotype) of Africans, which represents Africans as primitive, uncivilized, savage, barbaric, irrational, instinctual, passion-driven creatures. This stereotype biases the processing of information about African individuals and groups in such a way that Westerners perceive them as instances of the stereotype. That is, the stereotype serves as a template that governs each step of information processing. It leads people to *expect* that Africans will be irrational, uncivilized, and so on, to *overlook or discount* evidence to the contrary, to *focus on* and *search for* details that can be *interpreted* as evidence of these qualities, to simply *suppose* these details if they cannot be found, and to *encode* these details in memory as evidence of the supposed character traits.

This perception of Africans as primitive, uncivilized, savage, barbaric, irrational, instinctual, passion-driven creatures renders them subhuman, fundamentally different from, and hence possessing little or no overlap, sameness, or similarity with the Western perceiver, who consequently experiences little or no compassion for them and no motivation to help them. Studies of infrahumanization and dehumanization reveal that these judgments are produced by a contrast between one's prototype of the Other and one's prototype of the Human, and that the prototype of the Human generally coincides with one's prototype of one's own group. Psychologists have found that when two groups are members of a superordinate group (e.g., Poles and Germans are both Europeans, and Europeans and Africans are both Human), members of each group tend to generalize the distinctive properties of their own group to the superordinate category (e.g., Human). This generalization leads the ingroup (e.g., Europeans) to appear more prototypical of the superordinate group (e.g., Humans) than the outgroup (e.g., Africans) is. The outgroup is thus seen to deviate "from the prototype of the superordinate category" and is devalued as a result (Waldzus and Mummendey 467). As Waldzus,

Mummendey, and Wenzel explain, "If the in-group is more prototypical than the out-group, then the out-group deviates from the prototype of the superordinate category, [and] [t]his deviation justifies negative attitudes towards the out-group" (77).

Research has also revealed that, conversely, people who recognize their perceived oneness or overlap with the Other exhibit greater compassion and helping behaviors toward the Other (Cialdini et al. 489–492; Levy et al. 1224–1225). Several different laboratory studies based on various research models have shown that "hostility toward the outgroup is reduced ... when the outgroup is perceived as equally prototypical to this superordinate category" (Gaunt 734). And ethnographic studies of people who helped members of outgroups have found that perceived oneness, or common humanity, was a key cause of this behavior. Political scientist Kristen Monroe conducted in-depth interviews with rescuers of Jews during the Holocaust, philanthropists, and Carnegie Hero Commission Award recipients and found that all of these altruists "saw themselves as individuals strongly linked to others through a shared humanity" and that "their cognitive-perceptual frameworks differed consistently and significantly from those of traditional rational actors in this one regard" (Monroe 109). Monroe explains that while other factors have been put forward as explanations of altruism, they are not the crucial cause but rather mechanisms that trigger the perception of a shared humanity: "it is the perception of a shared humanity with the other that these external mechanisms trigger which remains critical, not the mechanisms themselves" (110). She concludes that it is the "perception of themselves as individuals strongly linked to others through a shared humanity ... that most successfully explains altruism. It is the only factor that consistently and systematically predicts altruism among all the individuals I interviewed" (110).

More generally, research has revealed that non-prejudiced people tend to operate with cognitive person-schemas that produce a "universalist orientation" to other people, "whereby perceivers selectively attend to, accentuate, and interpret similarities rather than differences between the self and others" (Phillips and Ziller 420). Stephen Phillips and Robert Ziller assessed the differing degrees to which individuals operate with a universalist orientation by having them indicate how strongly they agreed or disagreed with statements such as, "At one level of thinking we are all of a kind," "I can understand almost anyone because I'm a little like everyone," and "The same spirit dwells in everyone" (Phillips and

Ziller 422). They found that people who scored high on this Universalist Orientation Scale (UOS) "were just as accepting of minority targets as they were of nonminority targets, rating them as equally attractive, equally similar, and equally desirable as a potential work partner," that high-UOS individuals "found minority persons more representative of humankind and more attractive than participants scoring low on the UOS did, and that such individuals discriminate less on the basis of ethnicity" (427, 429). Phillips and Ziller conclude "that orientation to similarity between the self and other ... is critical to nonprejudice, whereas a difference orientation between self and other ... sets the stage for prejudice" (421). This is because

> universal orientation avoids the first treacherous act in interpersonal relations, that is, the separation of self and other, which tends to be followed by an invidious comparison of the self and other, to justify the separation. Through the simple act of orienting toward differences between self and others, the foundation is set for conflict rather than accord. ... Nonprejudice [in contrast,] begins with an orientation toward similarities between self and other, followed by an integration, or the perception of unity between the self and other even to the extent of seeing the self reflected in the other. (Phillips and Ziller 430)

Research has, in addition, revealed two basic forms in which outgroups are perceived to deviate from the category of the Human. The most common form involves denying that the Other possesses uniquely human (UH) qualities that distinguish humans from other animals, such as "cognitive sophistication, culture, refinement, socialization, and internalized moral sensibility," including "industriousness, inhibition, and self-control" (Haslam 256). The other form of dehumanization denies that the Other possesses certain qualities that are central to human nature (HN), such as interpersonal warmth, drive, and vivacity (257). The first, UH, mode of dehumanization characterizes the Western view of the Other, including Africans. Nick Haslam describes the various ways in which Westerners deny uniquely human attributes to their various Others:

> ethnic and racial others have been represented, both in popular culture and in scholarship, as barbarians who lack culture, self-restraint, moral sensibility, and cognitive capacity. Excesses often accompany these deficiencies: The savage has brutish appetites for violence and sex, is impulsive and prone to criminality, and can tolerate unusual amounts of pain. ... A consistent theme in this work is the likening of people to animals. In racist descriptions Africans are compared to apes and sometimes explicitly

denied membership of the human species. Other groups are compared to dogs, pigs, rats, parasites, or insects. Visual depictions caricature physical features to make ethnic others look animal-like. At other times, they are likened to children, their lack of rationality, shame, and sophistication seen patronizingly as innocence rather than bestiality. (Haslam 252–253)

Haslam notes that that the uniquely human characteristics that are denied to the Other also often include a distinct, individual identity that allows individuals in the outgroup to be distinguished from each other; agency, the ability to make choices and take effective action; community, or participation in a web of interpersonal relationships involving mutual care and concern; prosocial values, such as equality, helpfulness, and forgiveness, which demonstrate that the group has transcended animal hedonism; and certain "secondary" emotions, such as compassion, guilt, and shame, which are presumed not to exist among animals (254–255). Haslam reports that when people are perceived to lack any of these uniquely human emotions, values, or modes of being, they "lose the capacity to evoke compassion and moral emotions, and may be treated as means toward vicious ends. People who aggress [against them] are spared self-condemnation and empathic distress if their identification with [them] is blocked" by such dehumanizing perceptions (254).

This form of dehumanization leads to each of the three compassion- and aid-denying perceptions. Obviously, it profoundly reduces, if not eliminates entirely, any perception of sameness or overlap with the outgroup. But it also significantly reduces the perception of the outgroup's suffering, particularly emotional suffering, since animals are generally assumed not to suffer as intensely, either physically or emotionally, as humans (see Costello and Hodson 4). And this animalizing dehumanization also blocks the perception that the outgroup doesn't deserve its suffering or degraded state, since animals aren't thought to deserve a higher quality of life. As Costello and Hodson note, "Portrayals of outgroups as 'subhumans' who are less capable of experiencing emotions and/or pain render the outgroup less deserving of compassion and respect...in the same way that non-human animals are morally excluded for the purposes of exploitation by humans" (4). Thus insofar as "animals are already defined as lower-life fated for exploitation and slaughter, the designation of lesser humans as animals pave[s] the way for their subjugation and destruction" (Patterson; qtd. in Costello and Hodson 5).

Changing faulty person-schemas

One key to increasing the defining element of cosmopolitanism—helping distant others who are in need—is thus to increase people's recognition of their sameness and overlap with Others. Changing their habitual distorted—and sometimes dehumanizing—perception of Others, however, requires much more than evidence and logical argument. It requires replacing not just faulty propositional beliefs about Others but also multiple non-propositional forms of knowledge. These non-propositional forms of knowledge, as noted above, include prototypes, exemplars, and information-processing routines.

Prototypes, the most familiar form of which is the stereotype, are models incorporating what are taken to be the most typical features of members of a given category. Prototypes come in multiple forms, including concepts, prototypic individuals, prototypic body images, episode scripts, life scripts, prototypic emotions, and action scripts. Prototypes (including stereotypes) distort perception by automatically attributing all of the prototypical features to any individual who is perceived as belonging to that particular category.

Exemplars are individual instances of a particular category, and they occur in the same multiple forms as prototypes, which, in fact are formed out of exemplars when similar exemplars reach a critical mass. Exemplars function in the same way as prototypes, transferring their features to any given individual who is identified as a member of the same category.

Information-processing routines direct our expectations, attention, information search, inferences, suppositions, and emotional responses to other people, and any or all of these information-processing steps can be misdirected by our established, default routines.

Faulty prototypes of the Other

Each of these forms of non-propositional knowledge—prototypes, exemplars, and information-processing routines—can produce the perception that the Other bears no similarity to oneself and thus also facilitate the judgment that the Other is not suffering and/or that the Other deserves to suffer. Consider the various forms of the Western prototype of Africans and how they deny Westerners' sameness with Africans. *Concepts* used to describe Africans include negative terms of binary oppositions which have no overlap with their positive counterparts. These binary oppositions include civilized/uncivilized, rational/irrational, cultured/barbaric, adult/childlike, rational/irrational, and humane/savage. Describing Africans with the infra- and de-humanizing terms of these dichotomous pairs effectively denies their full humanity and obscures any significant sameness or overlap between Africans and Westerners.

Prototypic individual figures of Africans embody or invoke similar dichotomous oppositions between Africans and Westerners. One prime example is the African hunter, who is counterposed to the Western farmer, laborer, and entrepreneur (hunting in the West being no longer an occupation but rather a form of recreation or sport). Another example is the African warrior, which invokes, and is sometimes explicitly replaced by, the figure of the head-hunter or "spear-chucker," and which is counterposed to the Western soldier, who operates with sophisticated weaponry and technology.

These prototypic individuals are often supplemented by *prototypic body images* that also connote infra- or non-human status. Such images include men wearing only a loincloth or a penis sheath and bare-breasted women, with the lack of clothing being equated to lack of civilization and self-restraint. Other overlap-denying images include non-Western forms of makeup, jewelry, and body piercings, tattoos, scarifications, and distortions, as well as skin color and hair and facial features that contrast with their prototypical Caucasian counterparts.

Overlap between Africans and Westerners is further denied by the prototypic actions and events, or *episode scripts*, attributed to Africans by the Western stereotype. Prototypic episode scripts include hunting and foraging in the jungle with rudimentary (unsophisticated or "uncivilized") tools, implements, and techniques; warring with other tribes (rather than nations), dressed in war paint and animal parts (rather than camouflage uniforms and night vision goggles), using "primitive" weapons such as spears and blowguns (rather than automatic rifles, armored vehicles, aircraft, smart bombs, and drones), and emitting shrieking war cries while shaking spears and shields (rather than operating with sophisticated, "civilized" strategies and tactics); and ceremonies involving midnight dances to the beat of jungle drums in the light of a bonfire while dressed in "primitive" costumes and emitting "eerie" sounds (rather than more sedentary, "civilized" assemblies and strategy sessions). Prototypic episode scripts of Africans notably do not include any farming activities (clearing land, planting crops, cultivating them, irrigating them, harvesting them, storing them, caring for domesticated animals, etc.); fishing; preparing food to eat; caring for children; courting; making tools, implements, and weapons; building and repairing houses; or socializing or governing.

The *life scripts* attributed to Africans are similarly impoverished and overlap-obscuring. The prototypic African life story as embodied in the Western stereotype involves little planning, long-term projects, or collective projects; rather, the prototypical African life involves living in the moment, largely hand-to-mouth, guided by one's instincts. Pursuing personal ambitions and collective goals, raising children, aspiring and planning for their futures, and taking action to ensure those futures are entirely absent from the African life script embodied in the Western stereotype.

These various prototypes often function in concert, even interwoven with each other. And they are also mutually imbricated with the *prototypic emotions* of Westerners regarding Africans, with these emotions both resulting from and helping to produce the faulty judgment that Africans have little or nothing significant in common with Westerners. As we saw with compassion, emotions are products of one's appraisal of one's situation or the object of one's attention: when certain specific appraisals of the Other are made, a certain emotion will follow. The various Western prototypes of Africans produce certain prototypic emotions in Westerners because of the specific appraisals they produce. Thus Westerners feel indifference toward Africans because they perceive them as creatures who are beneath them, and they feel disdain, contempt, and even anger toward them insofar as they see them as not only as beneath them but as potentially infecting Westerners or contaminating them with their inferiority. Westerners feel disgust at the supposed bestial nature of Africans. Westerners feel fear and anger at Africans' supposed inclination, as bestial creatures, to do harm to Westerners. And at best, Westerners feel condescending pity concerning not just Africans' deprived state but also their supposed debased nature.

Such emotions are produced by the various prototypes just discussed, because these prototypes filter out, distort, and fabricate information about Africans in such a manner as to produce appraisals of Africans that result in the respective emotions. Conversely, these prototypic emotions themselves produce distorted information processing that leads to the judgment that Africans are a subspecies that has no significant sameness or overlap with Europeans. That is, these emotions not only result from the respective appraisals mentioned, but they also function to guide information processing toward such appraisals (see Oatley et al. 258–287 and Clore et al.). Fear, for example, orients one to expect, search for, focus on, infer, and suppose threats in the object of one's appraisal. Anger, similarly, prejudices one toward appraising others' intentions as harmful, and disdain, contempt, and disgust cause one to recoil from the Other, thus precluding the perception of other, more benign attributes that these people might embody. This mutual production of emotions and appraisals can result in a vicious circle in which faulty cognitive appraisals produce these unjust emotions, which in turn distort information processing in ways that reproduce the faulty appraisals, and so on.

And finally, the Western stereotype of Africans includes *action scripts*, prototypic ways of dealing with Africans. These actions follow naturally from the judgment (produced by the other prototypes we have just discussed) that Africans are subhuman and thus have little or no sameness or overlap with Westerners, a judgment that itself underlies the prototypic emotions, which serve as a source of the action scripts (because every emotion includes a specific action tendency as one of its essential components) and which also supply most if not all of the motive force behind the prototypic actions. These action scripts include ignoring and neglecting Africans, as the West has often done in response to famine and genocide there (in contrast to its response to similar events in Europe); outright exploitation, domination, and enslavement of Africa and Africans, of which there is a long and sordid history on the part of the West; and efforts to variously "civilize," convert, and "save" Africans from their debased lives—efforts that are at best ethnocentric and paternalistic and at worst a cover for, and another form of, exploitation and domination. Like emotions, action scripts do not just result from judgments, they also influence judgments, by embodying various forms of tacit knowledge (which can of course be false). They do so, first, by providing a cover of legitimacy and respectability for the judgments on which they are based. In addition, even when no action is taken, the ready accessibility of specific action scripts biases information processing in the direction of the judgments that underlie the action.

Because of these multiple forms of prototype knowledge contained in the Western stereotype of Africans, even if Westerners subscribe to the *proposition* that Africans are fully human, their perceptions, judgments, emotions, and actions (including public policies) regarding Africans will still be distorted by the implicit conviction, based in these various prototypes, that Africans are *not* as fully human as Westerners. That is, the various forms and elements of the prototypic African will continue to operate implicitly, beneath the threshold of consciousness, and will override Westerners' conscious, propositional knowledge and produce distorted, dehumanizing perceptions, judgments, emotions, and actions regarding Africans. This basic process has been documented many times with what is called aversive or modern racism, the often subtle and usually unconscious discrimination that many white Americans who hold antiracist values nonetheless still manifest toward African Americans (see Jones 124–130 and 150–160).

Correcting faulty information-processing structures

Preventing the dehumanizing and overlap-obscuring cognitions of the Other, then, requires more than just getting people to subscribe to correct propositional knowledge concerning the full humanity of the Other. It requires correcting each of the perception- and judgment-distorting prototypes of the Other that individuals hold. With regard to Westerners' cognitions of Africans, this means correcting each of the prototypes just discussed, since these generally have greater power in guiding information processing than propositional knowledge does (see Bracher, "Schema" and *Literature*). Several practices can contribute to correcting faulty prototypes. Most importantly, such correction requires the encoding in memory of powerful exemplars of Africans demonstrating their sameness with Westerners rather than just their differences. If individual exemplars of this sort are sufficiently salient and emotionally powerful, they can interfere with or even substitute for the faulty prototype in guiding information processing. In addition, when a critical mass of such exemplars is encoded in memory, they consolidate into a prototype of their own, which can replace the dehumanizing prototypes as the default templates guiding information processing about Africans.

Developing metacognition can also play a valuable role in correcting faulty prototypes: by becoming aware of their multiple forms of flawed prototypes of the Other and understanding how these prototypes operate automatically and outside their awareness, people can develop automatic cues to apprehend this process, interrupt it, and engage in conscious reappraisal of the Other—which actions can themselves become automatic with sufficient repetition. This metacognition, moreover, can include an awareness of each of the various information-processing steps that a thorough and more adequate assessment of the Other would require and then consciously initiate the enactment of each of these steps (see Wells 120ff.).

Literary texts as schema-altering apparatuses

Literature, unique among discourses in this regard, engages readers in each of these schema-altering processes,[3] and teachers who are aware of them and understand how they work can engage students in reading, interpretive, research, writing, discussion, and other activities in class and at home that reinforce these processes and thus contribute significantly to the correction of the three faulty judgments regarding the Other. One of the most basic and most important things teachers can do to promote these corrective processes is to select texts that provide multiple corrective exemplars for each of the prototype categories (prototypic individuals, prototypic body images, episode scripts, etc.). Simply having students read such texts, however, will not usually be sufficient to alter their faulty prototypes of the Other. For such a change to take place, students must, in addition to encountering the corrective exemplars in the text, also *recognize these textual elements as corrective exemplars and encode them as such in their memories*. Teachers can promote such recognition and encoding not only by framing the corrective exemplars as such for their students but also by instructing students to expect, search for, and focus on such corrective exemplars as they read the text, and by giving students writing assignments in which they describe these exemplars in detail and explain how they are more valid than the faulty prototypes they are countering. The encoding in memory can be further promoted by requiring students to recall these exemplars on exams—a practice that is enhanced by providing students with study questions before the exam that prompt them to encode these multiple corrective exemplars firmly in their memory so that they are readily accessible at exam time—and, more importantly, after the exam as well.

In addition, teachers can help students develop metacognition and correct their faulty information-processing routines through certain kinds of reading instructions and writing assignments. For reading, teachers can instruct their students to expect, search for, focus on, infer, and suppose the existence of information concerning the Other's full humanity and fundamental sameness with themselves—and also to be alert to their own emotions and action tendencies regarding the Other. Teachers can also have their students write about their actual, faulty information processing while reading a particular text, instructing them to notice, describe, and assess the adequacy of the various information-processing acts they engaged in while reading the text. One of the most effective ways for developing metacognition and correcting faulty information-processing routines is to have students keep a diary recording their cognitive encounters (in memory, in imagination, or in actuality, as well as in reading) with the Other, noting the information-processing routines (expectations, inference, supposition, etc.) that they activate in these encounters and assessing the accuracy and consequences of this processing—that is, identifying how the various information-processing acts they engage in work either to obscure or to apprehend the Other's humanity and sameness with themselves.[4]

When students have acquired a critical mass of corrective exemplars of the Other and have developed a certain degree of metacognition regarding their own information processing, their humanity- and sameness-recognizing information processing of the Other can be developed further by having them read texts that represent the Other in ways that obscure or even deny the Other's humanity and sameness with the reader. The reading and writing instructions for these texts should be to note the text's silences and distortions and to provide—through information search, inference, or supposition—the missing or corrective information concerning the Other's full humanity and overlap with oneself. Thus for reading Conrad's *Heart of Darkness*, students can be instructed to search for, infer, and/or suppose information about the Congolese people that demonstrate their full humanity and overlap with themselves. Such assignments can involve various deconstructive, psychoanalytic, Marxian, or historicist analyses, such as searching the text's margins for indications of the Other's humanity, inferring the Other's humanity and sameness with themselves from certain qualities or behaviors that the text attributes to the Other and/or to the protagonist's responses to the Other, or drawing on evidence from outside the text to correct the faulty prototypes promoted by the text. For all of these activities, the key is to look for self-other overlap, similarities, sameness.[5]

In the next chapter, we'll examine Chinua Achebe's classic novel *Things Fall Apart*, identifying the various resources the text offers for correcting Westerners' faulty schemas of Africans and also of themselves, and describing how to maximize these schema-correcting potentials with specific pedagogical strategies, practices, and assignments.

Notes

1. The term schema is sometimes defined more narrowly to mean abstract knowledge, in distinction from exemplars, prototypes, and information-processing routines. In adopting a broader, more inclusive definition of the term, I am following the usage of Taylor and Crocker, Moskowitz, and others.
2. For a discussion of when prototypes count as stereotypes and when they do not, see Hogan, *Conformism* 126.
3. Guy Cook argues that the basic function of literature is precisely to alter readers' cognitive schemas. His understanding of how literature does this, and the types of schemas it works on, differs from mine, however. Derek Attridge, in *The Singularity of Literature*, provides a description of the way literature can change readers' cognition of the Other that is quite compatible with my account of schema change, though it differs in its emphases. See especially 80–82 and 123–125.
4. The schema-correcting techniques described here are derived largely from Young et al.; Wells; Griffith; Padesky; Smucker and Niederee; and Sookman and Pinard.
5. Such an orientation runs counter to the emphasis on difference that has dominated the humanities in recent decades in reaction against the oppressive effects produced by universalist claims about human nature (see Pinker). But as Kwame Anthony Appiah, Patrick Colm Hogan, and others have pointed out, such oppression derives not from focusing on human universals but rather from *failing* to do so and focusing instead on *false* universals:

> no racist ever justified the enslavement of Africans or colonial rule in India on the basis of a claim that whites and nonwhites share universal human properties. Rather, they based their justifications on presumed differences among Europeans, Africans, and Indians, usually biological differences, but often cultural differences as well. Indeed, "liberal" racism and colonialism—with their paternalistic emphasis on leading the native out of primitive ways and into civilization—were always based on specifically culturalist differentialism.... [A]s Kwame Appiah has noted, what anticolonial opponents of universals "are objecting to" in these cases "is the posture that conceals [the] privileging of one national (or racial) tradition against others in false talk of the Human Condition.... [T]heir complaint is not with universalism at all. What they truly object to—and who would not?—is Eurocentric hegemony *posing* as universalism." (Hogan, "Literary" 38)

Indeed, as we have seen, far from being the *cure* for oppression, the denial of human universality, in the form of dehumanization, infrahumanization, and oblivion to self-other overlap, is actually a major *cause* of oppression, and any true cure must involve a recognition of the Other's common humanity and overlap with oneself.

Whenever two parties (individuals or groups) are compared, the sameness focused on should be instances of (or an entailment of) vital identity components of both parties, and all differences should be subsumed under these categories of sameness. This hierarchical relation between sameness and difference is in a sense always already operative in any discussion of difference, as Todorov indicates when he states: "The very idea of differences among societies or individuals implies qualities in common, and this communality makes comparisons and the study of differences fertile or at least possible" (ix). More substantively, truly recognizing and appreciating difference, as Taylor explains, means that we take the different ways of being to have equal value, which implies, in turn, a common ground on which the differences are judged to be of equal value:

> Mere difference can't itself be the ground of equal value.... If men and women are equal, it is not because they are different, but because overriding the difference are some properties, common or complementary, which are of equal value.... To come together on a mutual recognition of difference—that is, of the equal value of different identities—requires that we share more than a belief in this principle; we have to share some standards of value on which the identities concerned check out as equal. (Taylor 51–52)

Thus as Stevenson suggests, "the demand that we respect difference is dependent upon a hidden form of universalism rather than its negation" (Stevenson 265).

3
Correcting Ethnocentric Prototypes of Self and Other with Achebe's *Things Fall Apart*

Abstract: Things Fall Apart *promotes Western readers' recognition of their sameness with Africans by presenting African characters that Western readers can recognize as the same as themselves, along with European characters that possess negative traits that Westerners stereotypically ascribe to Africans but not to themselves. The novel also trains readers in more adequate information processing, by guiding and inducing them to repeatedly expect, attend to, infer, suppose, encode, and recall crucial information about self and Other—namely, negative qualities of Westerners and positive qualities of Africans—that their hegemonic prototypes cause them to routinely overlook, ignore, or discount. Teachers can engage students in specific reading and writing assignments that enhance their development of more the adequate information-processing routines and their acquisition of the more adequate exemplars.*

Mark Bracher. *Educating for Cosmopolitanism: Lessons from Cognitive Science and Literature.* New York: Palgrave Macmillan, 2013. DOI: 10.1057/9781137390202.

In teaching *Things Fall Apart*, many teachers, in line with the dominant trend in recent decades, have focused their students' attention on the differences between themselves and the Ibo characters in this novel.[1] The research on dehumanization cited in the previous chapter suggests that such an approach may be exactly the wrong one to take if one is trying to correct Westerners' faulty prototypes of Africans.[2] Such an approach would also appear to be antithetical to Achebe's intent, for one of his main goals in writing the novel appears to have been to lead Western readers to recognize their overlap and sameness with Africans. In "Teaching *Things Fall Apart*," he writes, "Africans are people in the same way that Americans, Europeans, Asians, and others are people. Africans are not some strange beings with unpronounceable names and impenetrable minds. Although the action in *Things Fall Apart* takes place in a setting with which most Americans are unfamiliar, the characters are normal people and their events are real human events" (Achebe, "Teaching" 21). In order for Westerners to recognize this fact, however, it is necessary to correct the "dehumanization of Africa and Africans" embodied in "the dominant image of Africa in the Western imagination" (Achebe, "Image" 1790, 1793), and whatever its author's intention, *Things Fall Apart* functions in multiple ways to accomplish just that.

The novel operates in several ways to make these corrections in Western readers' minds. Most significantly, it presents an array of exemplars that correct each of the dehumanizing prototypes of Africans described in the previous chapter in the direction of greater similarity with Westerners' prototypes for both Westerners specifically and the Human generally. That is, the novel presents characters that Western readers can recognize as the same as themselves and actions and events that Western readers can recognize as the same as their own. As Achebe observed, because at bottom Africans are "normal people," just like Westerners, "in spite of serious cultural differences, it is possible for readers in the West to identify, even deeply, with characters and situations in an African novel" (Achebe, "Teaching" 22). The most salient and emotionally compelling of these exemplars can themselves substitute for, or override, their corresponding faulty prototypes in guiding any particular instance of information processing about Africans. And as these corrective exemplars reach critical mass, they in turn begin to form new prototypes, and these new prototypes can, through repeated activation and pedagogical reinforcement, come to replace the dehumanizing, overlap-obscuring prototypes of the Western stereotype.

In addition, *Things Fall Apart* provides exemplars of Europeans that work to correct faulty prototypes that Westerners have of themselves. The flaw in this prototype—which largely coincides with Westerners' prototype of the Human—lies in the fact that it excludes the negative qualities possessed by Westerners as well as by humans in general. And this failure to recognize the negative qualities in oneself can be just as big an obstacle to recognizing self-other overlap as the failure to recognize the Other's positive qualities. Conversely, just as the failure to perceive self-other overlap can be produced either by the prototype of self or by the prototype of the Other, so also can perception of self-other overlap be enhanced from either direction: (1) characteristics attributed solely to the self can come to be recognized in the Other, and (2) characteristics attributed solely to the Other can come to be recognized in the self (Davis et al. 714; Galinsky et al. 118).

Things Fall Apart thus addresses the lack of overlap between Westerners' prototypes of themselves and their prototypes of Africans from both sides. On the one hand, it provides Westerners with exemplars of Africans that reveal them to be fully human (civilized, cultured, rational, humane, etc.)—quite like Westerners' prototypes of themselves and of the Human in general. It thus alters the African prototypes to overlap significantly with the (old) prototypes of the Westerner and the Human. And by the same token, the novel provides Western readers with exemplars of Europeans that reveal them to be primitive, savage, brutal, and irrational—much like the (old) Western prototypes of Africans. In this way, the novel alters the prototypes of Westerners and the Human in the direction of the Western stereotype of Africans as infrahuman. These new exemplars of Africans and Europeans thus work to move the Western prototypes of Africans and Europeans/Humans toward convergence, by (a) providing alternative exemplars of Africans that include positive qualities that the prototypes for Europeans (and the Human) include and that are normally attributed only to Europeans and denied to Africans, and (b) providing alternative exemplars of Europeans (and the Human) that include the negative qualities contained in the old stereotype of Africans and normally attributed only to Africans and other Others.

In addition to having students read *Things Fall Apart*, teachers can engage them in specific reading and writing assignments that enhance their apprehension and retention of these multiple more adequate exemplars of Africans. When I teach the novel, I ask my (overwhelmingly white middle- and working-class) students to do the following as they read:

1. Look for characters, characteristics, actions, behaviors, situations, events, artifacts, beliefs, values, mores, institutions, customs, and social structures that are similar to those of your own culture, and articulate the similarities for yourself.
2. Look for characters, characteristics, actions, behaviors, situations, events, artifacts, beliefs, values, mores, institutions, customs, and social structures that are unfamiliar to you and that may strike you as bizarre, irrational, immoral, or even inhuman. In each instance, ask yourself the following questions:
    a. Can I think of any present or past element of my own culture that is similar to this strange, disturbing element of the Ibo culture?
    b. What are the possible reasons for, and what are the likely consequences of, this element of Ibo culture? Can I think of any rational, logical reasons for its existence? Are there any benefits that derive from it?
    c. Can I think of any elements of my own culture that are or were the product of similar reasoning and/or that produce(d) similar positive or negative consequences?

Corrective exemplars

More valid prototypic individuals

The characters in *Things Fall Apart* are individual exemplars that as a group embody all of the qualities typically denied by dehumanization, including distinct individual identities, agency, community, prosocial values, socialization, culture, refinement, sophisticated cognition, internalized moral sensibility, inhibition, self-control, industriousness, humor, and uniquely human emotions such as compassion, guilt, and shame (Haslam 254–256). In the first place, in correction of the image of Africans as homogeneous masses whose members lack individual identity (an image perpetuated, as Achebe notes, by cultural texts such as *Heart of Darkness* [see Achebe, "Image"]), *Things Fall Apart* presents an array of characters who are as diverse and distinct as any group of Westerners. These differences are shown to result from the characters' distinctly different personalities, which also run the gamut of differences that characterize Westerners. Within a single family, for example, Okonkwo differs dramatically from both his father Unoka and his son Nwoye, not to mention from his wives and daughters, all of whom are also very different from each other. The novel's characters are also shown to be internally complex, occupying multiple social roles and motivated not by "the unspeakable craving in their hearts" that characterizes Conrad's (or at least Marlowe's) Congolese (Achebe, "Image" 1788) but by multiple and often conflicting feelings, desires, hopes, fears, and inhibitions, including uniquely human emotions such as compassion, guilt, and shame.

The protagonist Okonkwo is a particularly powerful exemplar of the full humanity of Africans in that on the surface he resembles the Western stereotype of the savage African: he is a fierce warrior and a literal headhunter, in possession of the heads of five enemies that he has killed in battle and from which he drinks wine, and he is also a violent, brutal savage off the field of battle, as he demonstrates when he beats his wives and children, fires his gun at one of his wives, beheads the messenger at the end of the novel, and, most of all, kills his beloved foster son Ikemefuna as the poor boy is seeking protection from him. On their face, these behaviors are more than adequate to confirm most features of the Western stereotype of Africans as amoral, uncivilized, subhuman creatures ruled by their impulses and instincts and totally lacking in properly human virtues and refinements. The novel makes it clear to readers, however—and teachers should emphasize this point—that Okonkwo's savage behaviors do not constitute a remotely accurate or complete picture of the type of person he is. Contrary to the Western stereotype, and to the colonialist texts that produce, reflect, and reinforce this stereotype, *Things Fall Apart* provides us with crucial information about Okonkwo that both contextualizes and explains his brutality. And this additional information about him that the novel supplies functions not just to produce a more complete account of his character but also to indicate and exemplify the kind of information that is systematically excluded from the representations of Africans that have dominated Western media for centuries up to and including the present.

This crucial but typically suppressed information is of two basic types. The first is behaviors that manifest what we think of as humanity as opposed to animality—behaviors of respect, self-restraint, inhibition, love, kindness, care, concern, generosity, empathy, compassion, pride, ambition, hope, envy, shame, and guilt. These more properly human and civilized qualities of Okonkwo are exhibited in his devotion to his daughter Ezinma, whom he cares for when she falls ill and whom he follows, at some peril to himself, when the priestess Chielo takes her away, over his protests, to the holy cave. They are also exhibited in his hard work, perseverance, and success as a yam farmer and in his efforts to maintain the integrity and viability of his clan in face of the onslaught by the European missionaries.

The second type of typically suppressed but crucial information supplied by the novel is that concerning Okonkwo's personality in general and his motives in particular. Most significant in this regard is the information that his most savage, brutal, and bestial behavior, far from being the manifestation of some overwhelming animal instincts that rule unchecked in the depths of his being, are instead the product of what is arguably individuals' most powerful—and most human—need: the need for identity, self-respect, recognition (see Bracher, *Social Symptoms*). The novel indicates quite explicitly that Okonkwo "was possessed by the fear of his father's contemptible life and shameful death" (18), and that in order to maintain an identity worthy of recognition and self-respect, he must therefore avoid those attributes of his father that brought shame and ridicule upon his father and, through his father, upon Okonkwo himself. Those attributes are failure, weakness, gentleness, cowardice, and idleness, and the novel indicates early on that Okonkwo's need to avoid them at all costs is the main cause of his violent, savage, "uncivilized" behavior:

> Okonkwo ruled his household with a heavy hand. His wives, especially the youngest, lived in perpetual fear of his fiery temper, and so did his little children. Perhaps down in his heart Okonkwo was not a cruel man. But his whole life was dominated by fear, the fear of failure and of weakness.... It was the fear of himself, lest he should be found to resemble his father. Even as a little boy he had resented his father's failure and weakness, and even now he still remembered how he had suffered when a playmate had told him that his father was *agbala*,...another name for a woman.... And so Okonkwo was ruled by one passion—to hate everything that his father Unoka had loved. One of those things was gentleness and another was idleness. (Achebe, *Things* 13)

These powerful psychological needs account not only for Okonkwo's quest for wealth, fame, and titles, but also for his anxiety about, and constant nagging and beating of, his son Nwoye for his "incipient laziness" and lack of masculinity (13–14), his arrogance concerning his own accomplishments (24, 31), his "brusqueness in dealing with less successful men" (26), and his suppression of his fondness for his daughter Ezinma (44) and of his affection for Ikemefuna on the grounds that "to show affection was a sign of weakness" (28). Okonkwo's psychological vulnerability and his consequent efforts to compensate for it are most evident precisely in those behaviors that are typically taken as evidence of someone's savagery, barbarity, and lack of humanity—particularly in his killing of his beloved foster son Ikemefuna as the boy runs to him for protection. As another man prepared to execute Ikemefuna by machete, "Okonkwo looked away. He heard the blow.... He heard Ikemefuna cry, 'My father, they have killed me!' as he ran towards him. *Dazed with fear*, Okonkwo drew his machete and cut him down. *He was afraid of being thought weak*" (61; emphasis added).

The fact that Okonkwo's violence and brutality are clearly the result not simply of brutal instincts but of profound psychological vulnerability not only demonstrates his humanity, it also constitutes a profound sameness with violent Western men, whose violent behavior has also been found to derive largely from the need to establish or protect their identity as men and thus avoid shame. Teachers can help students recognize this overlap with Westerners by first making sure they recognize that such brutal, savage behaviors are not unique to Africans but are unnervingly frequent in Western men as well. Some students will acknowledge this fact from personal experience or observation. Achebe reports, for example, that a white male student at the University of Massachusetts said to him, "That Okonkwo is like my father" (Achebe, "Teaching" 21). To make sure that students get the point, teachers can task them with finding published instances of Western brutality, whether from contemporary news reports or from historical accounts of war, colonialism, and slavery.

To help students recognize, furthermore, that the reasons for Okonkwo's violence are strikingly similar to the root causes of violent behaviors of Western men, teachers can share with their classes the findings of experts such as James Gilligan, who as head psychiatrist in the Massachusetts state prison system worked with hundreds of extremely violent offenders. Gilligan states:

> The emotion of shame is the primary or ultimate cause of all violence.... I have yet to see a serious act of violence that was not provoked by the experience of feeling shamed and humiliated, disrespected and ridiculed, and that did not represent the attempt to prevent or undo this "loss of face" ... [which]

is experienced subjectively as the death of the self. People will sacrifice anything to prevent the death and disintegration of their individual or group identity. (Gilligan 110, 97)

Men, Gilligan explains, are particularly vulnerable to this dynamic of shame and violence:

> Men are honored for activity (ultimately, violent activity); and they are dishonored for passivity (or pacifism), which renders them vulnerable to the charge of being a non-man. ... The male gender role generates violence by exposing men to shame if they are not violent, and rewarding them with honor when they are. ... Men ... are taught that to want love or care from others is to be passive, dependent, unaggressive and unambitious or, in short, unmanly. (Gilligan 231, 233, 237)

Helping students recognize how Gilligan's explanation, which covers Americans of multiple races and ethnicities, is an equally fitting account of Okonkwo's psychology can help them recognize an important dimension of their own overlap with Africans.

American students should have an easier time recognizing the full humanity of many of the other characters in the novel and also of detecting substantial similarities between these characters and themselves or people they are familiar with. The humanity of these and most of the other Ibo characters besides Okonkwo will be obvious and indisputable for most students, and it can be made plain by asking students simply to describe the characters. In doing so, they will use adjectives that clearly denote various human qualities and that also elicit associations with individuals and character types familiar in the West. Okonkwo's father Unoka will be recognized as a fairly typical ne'er-do-well, a gentle soul, ineffectual, improvident, and nonviolent (a "coward")—a kind of starving artist, a convivial musician who loves making music and drinking wine with his friends. Likewise, Okonkwo's son Nwoye, who resembles Unoka more than he does Okonkwo, is a sensitive and thoughtful boy who enjoys the women's stories more than Okonkwo's and who is deeply disturbed by the killing of his friend Ikemefuna as well as by the practice of abandoning infant twins in the Evil Forest. Ikemefuna himself is a friendly, smart, and knowledgeable boy universally beloved and admired—like a stereotypical all-American kid. The same is true of Okonkwo's ten-year-old daughter Ezinma, whose lively spirit elicits Okonkwo's admiration and his wish that she were a boy. Ekwefi, Ezinma's mother and Okonkwo's third wife, is a deeply sympathetic figure who has lost her first ten children and is profoundly devoted to Ezinma and romantically in love with Okonkwo, for whom she abandoned her first husband in order to be with the man she could not live without. Okonkwo's best friend Obierika is not only a man of admirable loyalty and generosity, he is also an individual with a philosophical bent and a keen critical mind who questions whether certain practices, such as the abandoning of infant twins and the exile of Okonkwo, are really justified. And Okonkwo's uncle Uchendu, from whom Okonkwo receives succor during his exile, is a dignified elder who has endured great suffering and achieved great wisdom. In addition to having students describe these characters, teachers can also promote the encoding of these characters as "just like me (or us)" by having students identify which characters are most like themselves or particular members of their families and then write a paper detailing all the similarities.

Teachers can also direct students' attention to the fact that, in contrast to stereotypical Africans, these characters not only speak but do so with a thoughtfulness, an insight, and at times an eloquence as well that is equal to that of their Western counterparts. Indeed, they cultivate their language skills, prizing the art of conversation and often speaking in proverbs (Achebe, *Things* 7). And they manifest all the uniquely human emotions as well. Ikemefuna's mother weeps bitterly when he is taken away from her, Okonkwo and Ekwefi manifest great anxiety and care when their daughter Ezinma falls ill as well as when she is taken captive by Chielo, Ekwefi falls in love with Okonkwo and follows her heart, and Okonkwo and his comrades feel deep shame and outrage when they are ambushed, taken prisoner, and subjected to bestial conditions by the District Commissioner. And the African characters are also shown to be eminently rational. In addition to the wisdom of Uchendu and the critical questioning of Obierika already mentioned, the entire village of Umuofia exhibits admirable rationality when, contrary to what their religion has taught them, the Evil Forest does not destroy the missionaries' church (149–151). In contrast to the rationalizations that most Western believers engage in when reality contradicts their beliefs, many of the Ibo people, with admirable empiricism and equanimity, begin to question their belief. They respond similarly to the Christians' challenge to their beliefs concerning the exclusion of outcasts and the killing of twins: when their gods don't punish them for associating with outcasts and keeping twins, they reasonably conclude that their beliefs are false and abandon them (155–157). Helping students articulate these counter-stereotypical facts explicitly will ensure that they are encoded as part of the corrective exemplars.

Teachers should also help their classes recognize and encode in memory how the European characters are anything but the paragons of rationality and fair-mindedness embodied in Westerners' prototypes of themselves. When the missionary Mr. Brown arrives in the village of Mbanta, he denounces the Ibo gods, accuses the Ibo of having "wicked ways," and threatens them with eternal torture if they don't renounce their gods and worship the Christian god—all without providing one shred of evidence or a single logical argument to support his claims (145–146). And when Okonkwo and his fellows, who have been listening to the missionary's claims, begin to draw a logical inference from them—namely, that if the Christian god has a son, he must also have a wife—the missionary and his interpreter ignore them and go on to talk about the Holy Trinity (147).

With a little priming, students can also recognize how Mr. Brown evinces the same dogmatism and irrationality in his discussion with Akunna comparing the Ibo and Christian religions. Whenever Akunna correctly notes a similarity between the two religions, Mr. Brown arrogantly and dogmatically rejects the idea, even going so far as to contradict basic Christian teachings and his own earlier pronouncements in order to do so and thus maintain the absolute separateness and superiority of Christianity in relation to the Ibo religion. When Akunna speaks of the Christian god in anthropomorphic terms, Mr. Brown admonishes him, "You should not think of Him as a person" (180) utterly oblivious to the fact that he himself has done exactly that in referring to his god as "Him" (as well as "Father" and "Son" at other times), and also quite forgetful of the fact that Christian theology defines the "Holy Trinity," about which Mr. Brown spoke earlier, as "god in three persons" and a "three-person godhead." And when Mr. Brown tries to further oppose the two religions by stating that in contrast to the Ibo god Chukwu, whom the Ibo feared, the Christian god "is a loving Father and need not be feared by those who do His will," he overlooks the fact that, as Akunna correctly points out, "we must fear Him when we are not doing His will... And who is to tell His will? It is too great to be known" (181)—a point made powerfully by Christianity's own Book of Job. Mr. Brown, who as a Christian missionary is an exemplary European, is thus revealed to be not nearly so rational and open-minded as Westerners' prototypes of themselves. And conversely, Akunna and the other Ibo embody considerably less irrationality and superstition than the Western stereotype of Africans claims.

In addition to being irrational, superstitious, dogmatic, and close-minded, the novel's Europeans are also arrogant, manipulative, scheming, treacherous, and brutal. Mr. Smith, the missionary who arrives when Mr. Brown has to leave for health reasons, is more rigid and dogmatic than his predecessor and is also quite moralistic and militant: "He condemned openly Mr. Brown's policy of compromise and accommodation.... He believed in slaying the prophets of Baal" (184). The District Commissioner, for his part, is both treacherous and obtuse. His treachery is on exhibit when Okonkwo and his fellows, having accepted his invitation to meet with him at his office, are ambushed, imprisoned, subjected to inhumane treatment, and held for ransom (193–196). His obtuseness is evident when, in the final scene, he views Okonkwo's suicide as but another curious detail demonstrating the savage and primitive nature of Africans (208–209).

Thus while the African exemplars are more rational and open-minded—and hence more human—than the Western stereotype depicts them as being, the European exemplars are more irrational, dogmatic, and close-minded than their own prototypes of themselves, and more like their stereotype of Africans. Teachers can help to establish these characters as exemplars of Westerners and Africans, respectively, by helping their students to explicitly articulate these points. And they can increase the force of the corrective exemplar of Westerners, and produce similar exemplars of the same sort, by engaging students in identifying and analyzing the District Commissioners and the Mr. Browns and Mr. Smiths in their own culture—government officials who, like the District Commissioner, are clueless concerning the destructive effects of their arbitrary and irrational policies and actions on the lives of ordinary people (and ignorant of the lives and character of these ordinary people), and Christian clerics and also laypersons who, like Mr. Brown and Mr. Smith, irrationally claim the existence of supernatural beings for which there is no evidence and further claim to have received instructions from these beings concerning how everyone else should live.

More accurate concepts

While various corrective concepts appear explicitly from time to time in the novel, most of them are implicit, embodied in the various characters, which is another reason that it is useful to have students describe the characters. Many of the terms used to describe the African characters will be concepts that counter the dehumanizing concepts at the center of the Western stereotype. These descriptors include, among others, the following: civil, kind, generous, loving, tender, considerate, contemplative, pensive, reflective, philosophical, wise, open-minded, empirical, rational, domestic, agrarian, and family-oriented. Descriptions of the European characters will also include many prototype-countering concepts, including ignorant, naïve, close-minded, dogmatic, defensive, irrational, self-delusional, arrogant, deceitful, treacherous, and brutal. Giving students the opportunity to utter and write these stereotype-countering descriptors will help insure their encoding in memory as part of the more accurate exemplars.

Humanized prototypic body images

While *Things Fall Apart* does not provide detailed descriptions of the bodies of either Africans or Europeans, it does provide a few salient exemplars of both types of bodies to counter the Othering and dehumanization of African bodies by the Western stereotype. As noted above, in the Western stereotype, African bodies are accorded various features that render them as unlike Western—and hence prototypically human—bodies as a body could be: unfamiliar facial features, expressions, piercings, scarifications, distortions, and makeup; bizarre movements, sounds, and dress; and partial—sometimes almost total—nakedness, all of which produce in Westerners the immediate perception of Africans as alien, animal-like, Other, not at all like "us." These bizarre-appearing body parts attract the Western gaze to themselves and away from the body as a whole, thus producing perceptual dismemberment of the African body that effectively denies its humanity. Conrad's presentation of African bodies in a *Heart of Darkness* passage commented on by Achebe functions in precisely this way:

> But suddenly, as we struggled round a bend [in the river], there would be a glimpse of rush walls, of peaked grass-roofs, a burst of yells, a whirl of black limbs, a mass of hands clapping, of feet stamping, of bodies swaying, of eyes rolling, under the droop of heavy and motionless foliage. The steamer toiled along slowly on the edge of the black and incomprehensible frenzy. (qtd. in Achebe, "Image" 1786)

Things Fall Apart counters such prototypic body images of Africans in part by eschewing detailed descriptions of characters' bodies and focusing readers' attention instead on their personhood—their personality and character, and the actions, events, and lives in which they are involved. And on those rare occasions when we do get descriptions of African bodies, they are whole bodies in motion, not curiosities on display for Western amazement or amusement, and the motion is reflective of their unique personality, as in the description of Okonkwo given at the beginning of the novel:

> He was tall and huge, and his bushy eyebrows and wide nose gave him a very severe look.... When he walked, his heels hardly touched the ground and he seemed to walk on springs, as if he was going to pounce on somebody. And he did pounce on people quite often. He had a slight stammer, and whenever he was angry and could not get his words out quickly enough, he would use his fists. (3–4)

The body of Okonkwo's gentle, lazy, improvident, and cowardly musician father Unoka similarly manifests his personality:

> He was tall but very thin and had a slight stoop. He wore a haggard and mournful look except when he was drinking or playing on his flute. He was very good on his flute, and his happiest moments were the two or three moons after the harvest when the village musicians brought down their instruments, hung above the fireplace. Unoka would play with them, his face beaming with blessedness and peace. (4)

Episode scripts of civilized behaviors

As noted above, the Western stereotype of Africans includes episode scripts—that is, typical actions and activities that they are imagined to engage in as a result of their supposed savage and uncivilized nature. Such episode scripts include fighting enemy tribes with spears and shields, dancing around a fire while making strange animal-like noises and movements in preparation for battle, and moving stealthily through the jungle, hunting wild animals with spears. But while Africans may have engaged in such activities from time to time, they were hardly typical, as even the slightest reflection or research would indicate. Achebe makes this point in his essay on *Heart of Darkness*, noting wryly "the abundant testimony about Conrad's savages which we could gather if we were so inclined from other sources and which might lead us to think that these people must have had other occupations besides merging into the evil forest or materializing out of it simply to plague Marlow and his dispirited band" ("Image" 1791–1792). *Things Fall Apart* provides multiple examples of these "other occupations," which can function as exemplary episodes to counter the faulty episode scripts of the Western stereotype, and which can themselves eventually combine into episode scripts to replace the currently dominant ones.

Two basic types of alternative exemplary episodes can be distinguished. One type is episodes that have clear Western counterparts, revealing Africans' sameness with Westerners and foregrounding Africans' humanity rather than their supposed inhumanity, their civilized rather than uncivilized nature, their rationality rather than irrationality, and their subjection to culture, society, ritual, ceremony, system, and restraint rather than to their natural, primitive, unbridled impulses and instincts. The second type of episode presents an action or activity that on its face seems quite inhumane and/or alien to the West but that upon reflection reveals itself to be fundamentally similar in its nature, motivation, or consequences to certain Western practices or events.

The first category of episodes includes rituals and ceremonies such as the Kola nut ceremony that takes place when one receives a guest into one's home (6), the meeting of the Tribal Council to determine whether or not to go to war (9–11), the elaborate negotiation of a marriage (69ff.), the settling of disputes through a trial before a panel of judges (88), the handing down of punishments for breaking laws (such as when Okonkwo breaks the peace), and the New Yam Festival held in celebration of the harvest (39ff.). Each of these episodes demonstrates that the Ibo are subjects of culture, society, and civilization and not creatures of nature, impulse, and instinct. These and other episodes reveal them to be people of mutual respect, cooperation, group loyalty, generosity, and love who recognize and adhere to various social roles, rules, ranks, and titles. Other episodes demonstrate sophisticated reasoning and critical thinking (e.g., Obierika's questioning of certain laws), language and story-telling skills (e.g., the story of the tortoise and the birds), and foresight and planning (e.g., the eschewing of a frontal assault on the Europeans and their followers because of the devastation of the Ibo clan that it would produce). Teachers can maximize the prototype-correcting potential of these exemplars by helping students recognize these implications in such episodes and encode them in their memory as prototypic African activities.

The second type of episode exemplar involves activities that strike Western readers as strange and bizarre, unlike anything with which they are familiar. These are the activities that often attract the greatest interest from students, as was the case with the high school student who wrote to Achebe that he "was particularly happy to learn [from *Things Fall Apart*] about the customs and superstitions of an African tribe" (Achebe, "Image" 1784). Noting that "The young fellow ... is obviously unaware that the life of his own tribesmen in Yonkers, New York, is full of odd customs and superstitions and, like everybody else in his culture, imagines that he needs a trip to Africa to encounter those things" ("Image" 1784), Achebe recommends that "It should be the pleasant task of the teacher, should he or she encounter that attitude, to spend a little time revealing to the class some of the quaint customs and superstitions prevalent in America" ("Teaching" 21). Numerous episodes in *Things Fall Apart* offer excellent opportunities to do just that. Indeed, many of these episodes seem to have been designed precisely to induce such realizations on the part of reflective readers, and the instruction, mentioned earlier, given to students to try to think of Western counterparts to any action, activity, or event in the novel that strikes them as bizarre or totally alien is enough for many students to identify such counterparts without further assistance.

Among the actions and activities that strike many Western students as inhumane, uncivilized, irrational, or incomprehensible are consulting an oracle to decide whether or not to go to war (9–11), killing Ikemefuna on orders from the oracle (57–61), delivering Ezinma up to the priestess Chielo upon demand (100ff.), Chielo's religious trance (106–107), leaving twins in the Evil Forest to die, abandoning the old and sick in the Evil Forest, the frenzied dancing to the beating of drums at the wrestling match (42ff.), the rendering of court decisions by masked ancestral spirits (*egwugwu*) (88), the distinction between male and female crimes, the exile of Okonkwo for an accidental shooting (125), and the practice of polygamy. Most classes are able, without much deliberation, to identify the same frenzied response to beating drums in a number of American activities, including dances, concerts, and high school and college football games, and they can fairly easily arrive at the insight that Americans have their own equivalents of polygamy, in premarital playing the field, extramarital affairs, and multiple serial marriages. And regarding Ibo legal practices, American students readily point out that the distinction between male and female laws is also found in Western law, only under the names of voluntary and involuntary manslaughter, and that Okonkwo's accidental killing of the boy when his gun explodes has its counterpart in the Western legal principle of negligence.

American students have greater difficulty in finding an American counterpart to the ancestral spirits who preside over court cases, but when prompted with the question of how many *egwugwu* there are (nine), followed by the question of whether a court with nine judges is found anywhere in American society, they begin to recognize a number of similarities with the Supreme Court, including costumes to disguise the individual identities of the judges and the pretense that the verdicts are rendered by ancestral spirits—for the Supreme Court, the Founding Fathers who framed the Constitution, as well as previous Supreme Court justices, in the form of the precedents established by their decisions.

Some students, presumably antiabortionists, propose that abortion is like the abandoning of twins to die in the Evil Forest. Students who do not make the highly problematic equation between a fetus (including a zygote) and a person, however, have a more difficult time finding parallels to this practice in America today, but when asked to reflect on the cause of the United States' high infant mortality rate, they recognize that the American system also engages in various forms of needless and inhumane abandonment of infants, including, for example, failing to provide necessary prenatal and neonatal care, not to mention inadequate childcare during later months and years. With this parallel in mind, students are usually able to see a similar abandonment of the old and ill in our society's equivalent of the Evil Forest, the nursing home.

The most difficult parallels to find are, for many students, those involving obedience to the oracle. Finding a Western counterpart to the most brutal and inhumane of these episodes, however, the killing of Ikemefuna, can be facilitated by asking students if they can think of any story in their culture of a father killing a son in response to orders from a higher power. Students with knowledge of the Bible will often recall the story of Abraham and Isaac, in which Abraham's willingness to kill his son in response to what he believes is a command from his god is seen as a virtue rather than a sign of savagery, inhumanity, or brutality. Some students will point out that Okonkwo's and Ekwefi's delivering their daughter Ezinma over to the priestess has even more disturbing equivalents in Western society, where thousands of parents, even in the absence of explicit demands, have for centuries delivered their children over to Catholic priests who have molested, raped, and otherwise abused them with, for the most part, not only impunity but also the awareness and apparent indifference of church officials up to and including the recently retired pope.

The idea of consulting an oracle to determine whether or not to go to war is recognized by some students as having counterparts in ancient Greece, but few are able to see anything similar in American society today. Here teachers can inform them that George W. Bush's decision to invade Iraq was, according to Bush himself, determined by precisely such a consultation: when asked by Bob Woodward whether he had consulted his father (former President George H. W. Bush, who had invaded Iraq a decade earlier) before deciding to invade Iraq, Bush replied that he had not consulted his actual father but had consulted a higher father—that is, his god. Asked to compare the consequences of the move advocated by Bush's higher authority and those of the action decreed by the Ibo oracle, students can come to recognize that while the Ibo oracle's decree ultimately produced one lost life (Ikemefuna's), the decree of Bush's god caused hundreds of thousands of deaths (when one includes the Iraqi deaths that resulted from the U.S. invasion), as well as countless mutilations, psychic traumas, untold suffering on the part of survivors, trillions of U.S. dollars, and possibly irreparable damage to the American economy—a comparison that might be said to render the Ibo considerably more rational, civilized, and humane than Americans today.

Such comparison of the humanity of Africans and Westerners is also invited by the portrayal of Europeans in *Things Fall Apart*. While the novel presents relatively few instances and details of European actions, the few that it provides constitute striking exemplars of irrationality, stupidity, superstition, treachery, savagery, and inhumanity. The most savage episode is the Europeans' massacre of the people of Abame. In retaliation for the killing of a white man whom Abame's oracle ordered to be killed as a threat to the village, the Europeans surround the village on market day and, waiting until the market is full, open fire, killing virtually everyone who is there (138–139).

European irrationality and superstition are revealed in the episodes in which the missionaries expound their theology, including the doctrine of the Trinity, which convinces Okonkwo that the missionary is insane (147). Students who have been raised as Christians may take exception to the notion that this doctrine is an instance of irrationality or superstition, much less madness, so it can be useful to have the class articulate the doctrine and recognize that it is mystifying even to believers. In addition to insisting that the Ibo accept this and other Christian doctrines (e.g., the notions of heaven and hell, and the idea that the Christian god is the only true god) on the basis of nothing more than his presumed authority, the European missionary, Mr. Brown, also exhibits self-contradiction, blatant indifference to evidence, and lack of logic, in the conversation with Akunna discussed above.

The two episodes involving the District Commissioner exemplify the treachery, inhumanity, and gross stupidity of Europeans. In the first, the Commissioner lures Okonkwo and his companions to the Commissioner's compound with an invitation to discuss their conflict. Okonkwo and his fellows arrive with open minds and good intentions, carrying only their machetes, dissuaded from bringing guns by the thought that such an act "would be unseemly" (193). When they enter the courthouse, they sheath their machetes, lay them on the floor, and sit down with the Commissioner. The Commissioner then calls in his men under the pretense of having them hear what the Ibo men have to say, and upon his signal, his men overpower the Ibo men, take them hostage, and hold them for ransom, during which time they torture and humiliate them by beating them, shaving their heads, refusing them water, and forcing them to urinate and defecate in their cell (193–195).

In his second episode, the Commissioner, upon being shown Okonkwo's body hanging from the tree behind his compound, in an act of gross stupidity and inhumanity that is, however, all too typical of Western responses to African tragedies, ignores Obierika's grief and rage over his friend's death, remains oblivious to his own contribution to it (despite Obierika's accusation that he, the Commissioner, has caused it), and then reduces it to a "detail" that "would make interesting reading" for other Europeans (208). Most students, having just read Achebe's story of Okonkwo's life and death, will be able to recognize fairly easily, with little or no prompting, just how inadequate, both intellectually and humanly, the Commissioner's understanding of Okonkwo is and thus to encode this episode as an exemplar of European obtuseness and inhumanity.

Humanized life scripts

The District Commissioner's book epitomizes the Western stereotype of African lives, the inadequacy of which is made abundantly clear by the book's title as well as by the stark contrast between the Commissioner's one-paragraph reduction of Okonkwo's life to the story of a "man who had killed a messenger and hanged himself" (208) and the novel-length account of this same life that the reader has just finished. The title of the Commissioner's book, *The Pacification of the Primitive Tribes of the Lower*

Correcting Ethnocentric Prototypes of Self and Other 43

Niger, embodies the Western stereotype of African lives as episodic, disjunctive, unorganized, and incoherent sequences of events, determined not by individual or group hopes, plans, strategies or projects, but resulting rather from wild, instinctual, and often violent reactions to whatever circumstances the jungle might confront the individual with on any given day. As a corrective to this Western life script, *Things Fall Apart* provides multiple exemplars of African lives having a unity, coherence, and trajectory created by the individuals' unique and complex personalities and plans. These life stories are much more than merely a hodgepodge of events and actions determined by external circumstances and instinctual reactions to them, and they often have counterparts in the life scripts of Westerners.

The prime example is the life of Okonkwo, which is the prototypic rags-to-riches, poor-boy-makes-good story that is so central to the American self-image. Okonkwo's motivation and back story also closely resemble Western prototypes: his ambition, motivation, work ethic, and perseverance, as noted earlier, derive in large measure from his childhood poverty and shame concerning his father, and virtually all his actions—including his striving to achieve ever higher social ranks and his wish for his children to do the same, as well as his periodic brutality toward his wives, his children, and men he perceives to be unmanly—are logical entailments of the character formed by his early life conditions.

A similar unified life story, deriving from the needs, plans, and coping strategies of a unique personality, can be seen in many of the other Ibo characters. Ekwefi, Okonkwo's second wife and Ezinma's mother, has lived a life with elements of Harlequin-like romance—running away from her husband to live with her true love Okonkwo (109)—followed by a long ordeal in which she lost nine children in infancy: "As she buried one child after another her sorrow gave way to despair and then to grim resignation. The birth of her children, which should be a woman's crowning glory, became for Ekwefi mere physical agony devoid of promise," bringing only a "deepening despair" (77). Then, when Ezinma survived beyond the age of three, "love returned once more to her mother, and, with love, anxiety," and Ekwefi devotes her life to her one surviving child's well-being: "She determined to nurse her child to health, and she put all her being into it" (79)—the prototypic devoted mother quite familiar to the West. As for Ekwefi's reason for living, Ezinma herself is the prototypic survivor who triumphs through struggle. At birth, "although ailing she seemed determined to live" (79), and throughout her childhood she has responded to her mother's care with "occasional spells of health during which [she] bubbled with energy like fresh palm-wine" (79), only suddenly to fall ill again.

The life of Okonkwo's father Unoka also follows a path well traveled in the West. His life of improvidence, debt, and shame, peppered with joyful episodes of conviviality, wine, and music, ends in an ignoble death that is too often also the fate of gentle souls in the West whose gregarious and peaceful temperament lacks the ambition and aggression that are so often prerequisites for conventional "success." The life of Okonkwo's son Nwoye—who, like Unoka, is a source of potential shame for Okonkwo—embodies another Western prototype, that of a son who clashes with his father as a result of their incompatible temperaments; questions the ways of his father and considers an alternative way of life; is chastised, punished, and abused by his father; and winds up abandoning his father and his father's ways and joining his father's enemies (152).

One final exemplary life, that of Okonkwo's uncle Uchendu, in whose village Okonkwo seeks refuge during his exile, fits the Western prototype of the wise, battle-scarred veteran, or graduate from the school of hard knocks. Uchendu's summation of his own life and life in general closely resembles the prototypic life of Greek tragedy, as well as the life of Job, as students familiar with Sophocles and the Bible will recognize. When Okonkwo is sulking in despair over his exile, Uchendu informs him of the number of wives and children he has lost (five and twenty-two, respectively) and of the multiple sets of twins his daughter has had to bear only to abandon, and he then recites for Okonkwo "the song they sing when a woman dies"—

> *For whom is it well, for whom is it well?*
> *There is no one for whom it is well* (135)—

which echoes the universal tragic life script articulated, for example, by the chorus's statement in *Oedipus at Colonus* that the best fate is never to be born and the next best fate is to die at birth, as well as by the chorus's lines at the end of *Oedipus Rex*:

> Let every man in mankind's frailty
> Consider his last day; and let none
> Presume on his good fortune until he find
> Life, at his death, a memory without pain. (1529)

Compassion and anger as the prototypic response emotions

The West's prototypic emotions for responding to Africans follow automatically from the assessment, promoted by the stereotype, that Africans are less than fully human creatures with little or no overlap with Westerners. These emotions include indifference for creatures who are beneath oneself and whose plight does not affect one's own condition; disdain and even contempt for them insofar as they are seen to presume to deserve one's consideration; disgust over their imagined uncivilized, bestial nature and activities; fear of their capability, as bestial creatures, to cause harm to oneself; anger over their supposed inclination to do so; and at best, a self-serving, condescending pity for creatures in such a deprived state and with such a debased nature.

Things Fall Apart, in contrast to the Western stereotype, evokes compassion for its African characters, along with empathic distress and, insofar as readers' collective identity as Westerners is salient, varying degrees of guilt and perhaps shame. The novel induces these emotions in its readers by leading them through the corresponding appraisals that produce them. The central appraisal for producing empathic distress and compassion, as explained earlier, is the recognition of the full humanity of the Ibo characters and hence of their sameness or overlap with oneself. The other key appraisals are the perception that the characters are suffering or in need, and the recognition that they are themselves not to blame (or at least not fully or ultimately) for this suffering or need. When readers make these three appraisals—usually automatically and outside of awareness—they feel compassion for characters who are suffering or in need. And when the Ibo characters' suffering is perceived as caused by the actions of the white characters, and white readers' collective identity as white is salient for them, these readers will also feel some guilt or shame regarding the suffering of the African characters. Thus when Okonkwo and his fellow villagers suffer severe losses to their yam crop as a result of drought and floods, after they have worked diligently to clear the land, plant the yams, and cultivate them, readers feel empathic distress and compassion for them, because their humanity and overlap with Westerners is evident in their identity as hardworking farmers, because loss of needed food makes their need abundantly clear, and because the need occurred through no fault of their own (since no farmer, even today, can control the weather). Such experiences of compassion establish memories of these African exemplars (characters, episodes, and life stories) that are infused with compassion, and these memories can produce compassionate responses to real Africans in two basic ways. First, when cognition of real Africans activates these exemplars in memory, the feeling of compassion that is part of these memories will be activated as well and will be transferred onto the present, actual Africans. Second, the feeling of compassion embodies within it the three appraisals that produce it, and as a result, the emotion of compassion biases information processing toward perceiving the other's humanity/overlap, need, and blamelessness, which appraisals will then further produce the compassion that (partially) produced them. The European characters in the novel similarly become emotion-infused exemplars in readers' memory that can similarly influence readers' future appraisals and emotional responses to actual Western imperialists and colonizers—the key emotions here being righteous indignation and moral anger, which are often companion to compassion.

Cosmopolitan action scripts

Together, the emotions of compassion and moral anger (and also guilt, when present) incline and motivate readers toward fundamentally different actions than the emotions infused in the Western stereotype of Africans. The prototypic actions, or action scripts, by which the West has dealt with Africans are clearly portrayed in *Things Fall Apart*. Under the euphemism of "pacification," the Europeans *invade* the "primitive" societies of Africa, attempt to *convert* the "irrational" and "superstitious" inhabitants to the "one true" god of Christianity, *control* the "violent" and "dangerous" natives by imposing European laws and *disciplining* and *punishing* (incarcerating) individuals who do not submit to their rule, and *exterminating* "the brutes" (Kurtz's words in *Heart of Darkness*) who forcefully resist European subjugation (such as the people of Abame). *Things Fall Apart* counters these action scripts not by providing alternative action exemplars of Europeans engaging in compassionate, humane actions toward Africans but rather by inducing emotional aversion in readers to these traditional action scripts together with an emotional inclination toward the action tendencies of assistance embodied in the compassion, moral anger, and guilt that we have just discussed. The emotional aversion is produced through readers' empathically experiencing the painful and unjust outcomes of the traditional action scripts, such as when the Europeans massacre the people of Abame, when Mr. Brown condemns Ibo beliefs and scoffs at Akunna's suggestions of similarities between those beliefs and Christianity, and when the Commissioner ambushes Okonkwo and his companions and subjects them to various forms of humiliation and torture. Events such as these evoke compassion and moral anger in readers, and these emotions, like all emotions, include a specific action tendency (Lazarus, *Emotion* 210). And since, as we have seen, the action tendency for compassion "is the impulse to reach out to mitigate the other's plight, to help the other person" (Lazarus, *Emotion* 290), compassion entails action scripts of helping the other. Similarly, the action tendency of opposition and resistance that is inherent in anger leads to action scripts of justified aggression against whoever may be harming the other.

Things Fall Apart thus works on multiple schema elements to enable Western readers to realize that Africans are just like (our idealized prototype for) "us": "they" have the same basic needs (food, water, shelter, respect, identity, society, love), the same basic vulnerabilities (bodily injury, illness, social exclusion, loss of loved ones, death, etc.), the same basic virtues and abilities (intelligence, courage, wisdom, etc.), and the same intra- and inter-personal diversity, complexity, and tensions. And the novel's exemplars of Europeans as irrational, savage, treacherous, and brutal enable Western readers to recognize that "we" are just like (our negative, distorted prototypes of) "them": violent, brutal, selfish, close-minded, irrational, superstitious, and so on.

In addition to helping students identify these various corrective exemplars of Africans and Europeans and fully apprehend the truths they exemplify about each group, teachers can take two additional important steps to promote the use of these more accurate information-processing templates in real life. First, they can make sure that these exemplars are firmly encoded *as corrective exemplars* in students' memories. To do so, teachers, in addition to employing the pedagogical practices already mentioned to this end, can have their students recall these exemplars on quizzes and exams and explain what they exemplify about each group. And they can also give students assignments that engage them in using these corrective exemplars to process information they encounter in the world outside the text, whether it be in other literary texts (including movies and television programs), in historical texts, in media reports, or in direct personal encounters. One such assignment is to have students find real individuals, actions, activities, and lives that resemble one or more of the novel's exemplars and explain the similarities between the fictional exemplar and the real person.

Training in more adequate information-processing routines

In presenting these alternative exemplars, *Things Fall Apart* also trains readers in more adequate information processing—by guiding and inducing them to repeatedly expect, attend to, infer, suppose, encode, and recall crucial information about self and Other—namely, negative qualities of Westerners and positive qualities of Africans—that their hegemonic prototypes cause them to routinely overlook, ignore, or discount. This training occurs through readers' repeatedly encountering African characters, actions, activities, and lives with a range of degrees of similarity with Western ones. After perceiving multiple such instances of sameness, readers begin to *expect* such sameness from the African characters, actions, and events, which means they pay more *attention* to the sameness when they perceive it, *encode* it in memory, and *recall* it from memory. And with enough repetition, they will also begin to *search for* such sameness when, expecting it, they don't see it.[3] As stated earlier, teachers can promote the development of such sameness-apprehending information-processing routines by instructing students to engage in them and by assigning the task of listing and explaining as many similarities as they can between the Ibo characters and members of their own culture.

In addition, teachers can instruct students to seek such sameness by conceiving apparently dissimilar persons, actions, and activities in more abstract terms. Noting that "when defined abstractly, the goals people pursue...appear universal across cultures and time periods," psychologists Sheri Levy, Antonio Freitas, and Peter Salovey found that "people who chronically represent action in abstract terms are more likely to view themselves as sharing goals with others and, hence, more likely to perceive similarity between themselves and others" (1224–1225). Thus, for example, if students consider the Ibo practice of consulting an oracle and their own culture's practice of praying to a god merely on their own terms, they will see no similarity between the two. But if they see both practices more abstractly, as consulting a higher power that they believe in, the similarities are obvious and compelling. Helping students develop the habit of conceptualizing their own and others' actions and activities in terms of fundamental and universal human qualities and needs will enable them to recognize the sameness of two actions, activities, or persons that appear quite different from each other—recognizing, for example, that chairing a meeting of the board of a major corporation and planting yams are both ways to procure food for oneself and one's family (see Levy et al. 1225). Similarly, leaving one's elders in the Evil Forest and putting one's parents in a nursing home produce the same results: freeing the young from the burden of caring for the old and infirm and from the pain of watching them suffer and die.

Acquiring these corrective exemplars and developing more adequate information-processing routines make it much more likely that Western students will arrive at the three compassion-producing appraisals when considering Africans outside the text. First and most obviously, these new cognitive capabilities will facilitate the students' perception of Africans' humanity and of other, more specific instances of overlap between themselves and Africans. Second, this recognition that "they are fundamentally just like me" will, in turn, make it easier for Western students to perceive the suffering or need of Africans where it exists, because they will no longer be able to assume that Africans are less human and thus not as sensitive to conditions that would cause Westerners to suffer. And third, apprehending Africans' ultimate sameness with themselves will also make it easier for Western students to recognize that Africans don't deserve their suffering any more than the students themselves would.

Notes

1 Nichols, for example, has his students "talk about the dangers of universalizing human experience on the basis of apparent similarities." As a result of such discussions, although his "students often start out wanting to blur the distinctions between Ibo and Western life," they eventually "move toward a view that accepts and appreciates difference. At the beginning they try to find Western parallels for every aspect of life in Umuofia, but they end up deciding that Nigerian village culture does not exist to be subsumed under a Westernized set of values and assumptions" (55–56). While such conclusions are true enough, they can easily lead to the inference that the differences between Ibos and Westerners are more important than the sameness, and from there to the obscuring of the Other's common humanity.

2 I will be speaking of Achebe's characters as Africans instead of Ibos, since this is Achebe's practice when discussing his novel in his essays and interviews. While this practice involves a homogenization of many subcategories of Africans, such homogenization would occur even if the subcategories were used instead; it occurs (as Hegel, for instance, noted) whenever one employs

any categories, including the subordinate categories (Nigerians, Congolese, etc.). Furthermore, such homogenization is not always harmful; indeed, it can be positive, as when it emphasizes real similarities or sameness between individuals or subcategories of individuals. Moreover, when certain categories (such as African and European) have wide currency and embody significant harmful distortions, it is important to rework these categories rather than attempting simply to bypass them. This is what Achebe himself does in *Things Fall Apart*, which he spoke of as working to correct mistaken European views of Africa and Africans, even though the novel is about a subcategory of Africans (the Ibo people).
3 On the development of new information-processing routines, and the importance of repetition, see Wells (90 and passim).

4
Developing Metacognition of Ethnocentrism with Lessing's "The Old Chief Mshlanga" and Voltaire's *Candide*

Abstract: *The accurate perception of the Other can also be enhanced through the development of metacognition, the awareness, understanding, and control of one's own cognitive structures and processes and their consequences. "Mshlanga" is an excellent text for promoting metacognition of ethnocentrism because it models the development of such metacognition and also portrays the causes, operations, consequences, and processes for correcting ethnocentric cognition.* Candide *provides numerous episodes of ethnocentrism distorting perception of self and Other. With such episodes serving as exemplars of ethnocentric information processing, teachers can help their students learn to recognize the same cognitive processes underlying not only the actual historical realities that Voltaire is alluding to but also current beliefs and practices, including the students' own.*

Mark Bracher. *Educating for Cosmopolitanism: Lessons from Cognitive Science and Literature.* New York: Palgrave Macmillan, 2013. DOI: 10.1057/9781137390202.

Metacognition, the awareness of one's own cognitive structures and processes—including their origins, their functions, and their consequences—can be a crucial element in the establishment of more adequate cognitive schemas of self and other.[1] For one, such awareness can initiate cognitive dissonance, a disturbing sense of an internal contradiction between two mutually incompatible perceptions, values, beliefs, identity contents, or behaviors. And cognitive dissonance, as an aversive state of mind, is a powerful motive to change one's mind, one's behavior, or both.[2] Metacognition of ethnocentrism—awareness of how one's cognitive structures and processes are biased and thus produce faulty perceptions and judgments of self and Other, which result in harmful and unjust actions—can thus be a valuable aid in replacing faulty, ethnocentric information processing with corrective, cosmopolitan cognition.

Literary study can promote metacognition of ethnocentrism in various ways. The ending of *Things Fall Apart* offers one such opportunity. As one commentator has observed, the novel's final paragraph forces readers to confront the fact that "[their] very perceptions are shaped by the social and cultural content out of which [they] operat[e]." Achebe himself agrees, stating, "That about sums up the mission of *Things Fall Apart*, if a novel could be said to have a mission" (Achebe, "Teaching" 23–24). The novel's final paragraph promotes metacognition in readers by presenting an instance of the Western misunderstanding of Africans that is so glaring and egregious that even the most obtuse reader cannot fail to register it. Having just read a novel about Okonkwo in which the complexity and humanity of the man have been demonstrated again and again, readers cannot help but recognize both the gross inadequacy of the Commissioner's assessment of Okonkwo and the Commissioner's total lack of awareness of his own faulty social information processing concerning Okonkwo specifically and Africans in general. The fact that even after "many years" in Africa the Commissioner is still "toil[ing] to bring civilization" to it indicates that his initial expectation of finding only "primitive tribes" in need of "pacification" has utterly blinded him to the fact that Africans already possess civilization. Although he has "learned a number of things" during his time there, the fact that he has remained completely ignorant of Africans' humanity demonstrates the power of Western prototypes to block out and cause people to ignore and discount all disconfirming evidence and, conversely, to infer and suppose various instances of confirming evidence. Rather than accumulating corrective exemplars as readers of Achebe's novel have done, the Commissioner—operating, with a complete lack of metacognition, out of his Eurocentric prototypes—has acquired only knowledge of how to manipulate and subjugate Africans.

Teachers can promote Western students' metacognition of their own information-processing activities by helping them spell out the Commissioner's information-processing flaws and recognize the same flaws in other Western (including students' own) information processing concerning Africans and other Others. Asked to reflect on how the Commissioner's faulty prototypes of Africans, acquired before he ever arrived on the continent, would have prevented him from recognizing their humanity and civilization for all these years, students can be prompted to notice and articulate how his *attention* and *information search* are directed only toward "details" and "new material" that he can *interpret* as evidence of primitiveness, and how he *ignores* or *discounts* contrary evidence even when he directly encounters it with his own eyes (e.g., in the form of the "dangling body" of Okonkwo) and ears (e.g., in the form of Obierika's declaration to him that Okonkwo was "one of the greatest men in Umuofia") (208–209). Understood in this way, the Commissioner's faulty information processing can then be offered to students as a touchstone for errors to avoid in their own processing of information about Others.

"The Old Chief Mshlanga"

A fuller battery of resources for developing students' metacognition of their perception and judgment of the Other can be found in Doris Lessing's short story "The Old Chief Mshlanga." Lessing's story describes how a white girl living in Africa, after recognizing the humanity of an old African chief on a chance encounter with him, and after seeing the devastation that her father and the other European settlers have wrought on Africans and the African landscape, comes to the realization that it is her people, not the Africans, who are deficient in humanity and civilization. The text demonstrates five key points regarding the operation of faulty cognitive schemas of the Other:

1 how such schemas operate;
2 how they are inculcated;
3 the fact that they are faulty;

4 what their cognitive, emotional, behavioral, and social consequences are; and
5 how they can be corrected.

How ethnocentric cognitive schemas work

The story begins by describing the effect of the small girl's Eurocentric schemas on her perception of the African landscape and its people. Her eyes, readers are told, "were sightless for anything but a pale willowed river, a pale gleaming castle" (1476). The leaves of the mealie stalks evoke in her mind not their own qualities but rather European cathedrals, and the "witchweed would summon up a black bent figure croaking premonitions: the Northern witch, bred of cold Northern forests, would stand before her among the mealie fields, and it was the mealie fields that faded and fled, leaving her among the gnarled roots of an oak, snow falling thick and soft and white, the woodcutter's fire glowing red welcome through crowding tree trunks" (1476). The narrator explicitly marks the power of the Eurocentric prototypes to blind the child to the physical realities in front of her: "A white child, opening its eyes curiously on a sun-suffused landscape, a gaunt and violent landscape, might be supposed to accept it as her own, to make the msasa trees and the thorn trees as familiars, to feel her blood running free and responsive to the swing of the seasons." But "this child," we are told, "could not see the msasa tree, or the thorn, for what they were" (1476). Nor could she see the African people as they were: "The black people on the farm were as remote as the trees and the rocks. They were an amorphous black mass, mingling and thinning and massing like tadpoles, faceless" (1477). The girl can't see the landscape or the people in front of her because she perceives, thinks, and imagines through the templates of her European prototypes.

How schemas of the Other are inculcated

The opening pages of the story also clearly indicate the sources of this cognitive dominance of the girl's ethnocentric schemas. The first source mentioned is books:

> This child could not see a msasa tree, or the thorn, for what they were. Her books held tales of alien fairies, her rivers ran slow and peaceful, and she knew the shape of the leaves of an ash or an oak, the names of the little creatures that lived in English streams, when the words "the veld" meant strangeness, though she could remember nothing else. Because of this, for

many years, it was the veld that seemed unreal: the sun was a foreign sun, and the wind spoke a strange language. (1476–1477)

The Eurocentric schemas of Africans are also inculcated through the admonitions and behaviors of her elders and her peers, and supported by the coerced conformity of the Africans themselves to these schemas. "The child was taught to take them [the African people] for granted: the servants in the house would come running a hundred yards to pick up a book if she dropped it. She was called 'Nkosikaas'—Chieftainess, even by the black children her own age" (1477). When white children got together, they would amuse themselves by setting the dogs on Africans they encountered and watching them run, and they would torment small black children for amusement, not only teasing them but also throwing stones and sticks at them with no sense of guilt (1477). In addition, the behavior of the girl's elders produced an "instilled consciousness of danger, of something unpleasant," associated with Africans. If the girl talked to one of the Africans, "her mother would come running anxiously: 'You mustn't talk to natives'" (1477). And in each case, the Africans' assumed lack of full humanity was reinforced in the biased European minds by the undignified, subservient, and sometimes frantic behaviors that the Europeans' behaviors coerced in the Africans.

The faultiness of the schemas

The most crucial form of metacognition regarding ethnocentric schemas is the recognition of their faultiness, for without such recognition and the cognitive dissonance it produces, there will be little or no motivation to free oneself from them. "Mshlanga" portrays how exemplars of the Other's dignity and humanity can begin to erode the chauvinistic, ethnocentric schemas. One source of this evidence is direct, first-hand contact with the Other under circumstances that make these schema-disconfirming qualities salient. Another source is own-group authorities who themselves may harbor the faulty schemas but whose discourse on the Other reveals, perhaps unwittingly, the Other's dignity and humanity. The narrator of the story has the crucial contact when, as a girl of fourteen, walking along a mealie field with her dogs, she sees three African men approaching her at a distance. She expects that they will step off the path as soon as they see her, as Africans generally do in deference to a white person. When they do not, the girl becomes angry. But then, as they draw nearer, she notices that this group is unusual, in that they are not seeking work and that they have "an air of dignity, of quietly following their own purpose" (1478). This air of dignity and purposefulness—evidence of their common humanity—strikes her and causes her to bite her tongue and refrain from chastising them. Instead, she asks where they are going, and when one of the two younger men indicates that the elder man is a chief, her ethnocentric schema of Africans is further eroded: "A chief, I thought, understanding the pride that made the old man stand before me like an equal—more than an equal, for he showed courtesy, and I showed none" (1478).

Teachers may ask their students to reflect on similar encounters they may have had with certain Others and to search for evidence of human purposefulness, dignity, and/or other indicators of their common humanity or overlap with themselves. And students may also be asked to reflect on whether they recognized these qualities in the Other at the time of encounter (and why, or why not), and if they did recognize them, if this recognition made them cognizant of the faultiness of their schema of the Other.

The schema-disconfirming worthiness and humanity of Chief Mshlanga is reinforced soon afterward by an old book written by an early European explorer of the region who referred to the land as Chief Mshlanga's country and spoke of his intention to ask the chief's permission to look for gold there. These ways of speaking about an African further undermine the girl's Eurocentric schemas and produce a significant cognitive dissonance in her: "The phrase 'ask his permission' was so extraordinary to a white child, brought up to consider all natives as things to use, that it revived those questions which could not be suppressed; they fermented slowly in the mind" (1479).

Teachers can help their students develop metacognition concerning similar tacit recognitions of truths about Others that are denied by their personal and cultural discourses. The first stage of such metacognition is the awareness of faulty, dehumanizing labels, representations, and generalizations concerning the Other. "Mshlanga" offers some obvious examples, such as the labeling of African natives as "raw black savages" and "damned niggers" (1480). Students will have little difficulty in calling to mind similar, perhaps only slightly less offensive, labels of Others circulating in contemporary American culture. The second stage of metacognition, exemplified in the narrator's proto-deconstructive reading of the discourses of old explorers and miners, involves finding implicit acknowledgment in the discourse's margins or between its lines, of the

Other's sameness and humanity. Attaining this stage of metacognition is more challenging for both teachers and students. It requires finding evidence of the Other's common humanity in texts or discourses where it is ignored or assumed not to exist. And it may even require recognizing how our ways of speaking about the Other offer evidence of the Other's humanity that we aren't aware of and may actually be in denial of. One obvious example is Americans' labeling of the 9/11 attackers cowards when they sacrificed their lives for their cause, while labeling Americans who do the same heroes.

Harmful consequences of the schemas

In addition to understanding the nature of one's mindsets, perceiving their effects on one's perception, judgment, emotions, and behaviors, and apprehending their faultiness, a robust metacognition also involves recognition of the consequences of these processes. Here too, "Mshlanga" provides important resources, modeling the development of this aspect of metacognition in the narrator-protagonist as she becomes aware of the physical and psychological suffering and injustice that the European schemas cause for Africans. The story portrays, in several episodes, the narrator's growing recognition of how the Eurocentric mindsets lead to physical suffering such as the Africans' loss of their homes, their land, their livestock, and their livelihood; of how these physical losses entail social losses such as the disintegration of their communities and families; and of how the physical and social losses together produce severe psychological consequences, including loss of dignity, self-respect, and identity.

In the first of these episodes, the narrator, having learned that her family's young African cook is actually the chief's son—and hence the future chief himself—and thus has another, very different life beyond his subservient role in their household, sets out to find Chief Mshlanga's kraal. As she leaves her family's farm and enters land untouched by Europeans, she feels that she has "entered a completely fresh type of landscape" (1480). This landscape features a small sparkling river in a lush green valley populated by tall trees, thick grass, and waterfowl. The landscape of her family's farm, in contrast, bears the consequences of the environmental rape and pillage practiced by the European settlers: its "hundreds of acres of harsh eroded soil bore trees that had been cut for the mine furnaces and had grown thin and twisted, where the cattle had dragged the grass flat, leaving innumerable criss-crossing trails that deepened each season into gullies, under the force of the rains" (1480). This encounter with the destruction wrought by her own people constitutes a body blow to her Eurocentrism and its sense of moral superiority and entitlement, and it leaves her feeling totally disoriented, confronted by an African landscape that far exceeds her and her people's capacity or right to dominate or control it. She experiences a growing anxiety that rises to a panic attack as she now sees herself no longer as a member of a dominant and morally superior group but rather as a creature utterly vulnerable to the landscape and the sometimes lethal other creatures that inhabit it, as well as being herself a member of a morally challenged species (1481).

Her encounter with the chief and his village further reveals to her the negative consequences of European "culture," as well as the profound inaccuracies in the European schemas of Africans. When, coming over a hill, she spots the village below her, she is impressed by its lovely, pastoral appearance: "There were neat patches of mealies and pumpkins and millet, and cattle grazed under some trees at a distance. Fowls scratched among the huts, dogs lay sleeping on the grass, and goats friezed a *kopje* that jutted up beyond a tributary of the river lying like an enclosing arm around the village" (1481). Drawing closer, she notices that "the huts were lovingly decorated with patterns of yellow and red and ochre mud on the walls; and the thatch was tied in place with plaits of straw" (1481). The contrast of these accommodations, produced by the African natives themselves, with those provided for them by the European settlers who employed them is striking: "This was not at all like our farm compound, a dirty and neglected place, a temporary home for migrants who had no roots in it" (1482). The settlers' accommodations for the natives deny their culture, civilization, and humanity that are so evident in their village and treat them as the "raw black savages" and "damned niggers" (1480) that European schemas egregiously take them to be.

The narrator's dawning awareness of the harm done to Africa and Africans by her own people, as well as of the inflated nature of her white sense of self, receives a further nudge when she notices that the chief is not pleased to see her. And when she observes that the only men present in the village are old, she realizes that "the young men were all away working on the white men's farms and mines" (1482), a fact that embodies the destruction wrought by the Europeans on African families, communities, and culture. As she leaves the village, which she now recognizes as "indifferent" (1482) to, rather than enamored of, her existence, she again notices the beauty and pastoral quality of the landscape with its "staring amber-eyed goats," its "tall stately trees," and its "great rich green valley where the river meandered and the pigeons cooed tales of plenty and the woodpecker tapped softly" (1482). And this time she hears the land's message loud and clear: "it seemed to say to me: you walk here as a destroyer" (1483).

Teachers might help their students achieve a similar metacognition by asking them to listen for a similar message from the American landscape and its history, directing their attention to the similar ways that European settlers on this continent took the land from its indigenous inhabitants and in many cases destroyed it and them. Having students research and report on the societies and cultures of various indigenous peoples will reveal ways in which some of them were clearly more fair and humane than the Euro-American culture and society that replaced them. The idea that American society and culture may be in some way inferior to others is unthinkable for many Americans, and to help students consider this possibility, teachers may wish to draw on authoritative Euro-American voices that have made this point. One brief, powerful statement of this sort can be found in a vignette in Steinbeck's *The Grapes of Wrath*, in which a migrant worker recounts an incident in which he and other cavalrymen shot and killed a magnificent Apache brave who was standing on a distant hill with his arms open to the sun, like Jesus on the cross. The ex-cavalryman reports that when he saw the brave's lifeless bullet-riddled body, he had the sense that he had killed something better than himself and in doing so had killed a part of himself as well (Steinbeck 325–326). Having students read and reflect on this page from Steinbeck's novel can help them entertain the notion that, like the protagonist of Lessing's story, they too walk here as destroyers. Teachers can also ask them to identify other ways in which they may be said to walk the earth as destroyers. Here students can reflect on various effects of U.S. foreign policy, including its military actions and economic policies. And then, by asking them to imagine how they would feel if the tables were turned and they were on the receiving end of such actions by another country, teachers may bring them to see how these policies are underwritten by distorted schemas of self and Other which accord certain entitlements to Americans that are denied to members of other nations, cultures, and ethnicities.

In the next episode in "The Old Chief Mshlanga," the destructiveness of the European schemas of self and Other is even more immediate, embodied in the disrespectful, authoritarian, and pitiless attitude and actions of the narrator's own father toward Chief Mshlanga and his people. One night the chief's goats trample over her father's farm, and her father takes possession of the goats, telling Chief Mshlanga that he will have to pay for the damage in order to get the goats back. Since the chief cannot pay the money, her father declares that he is entitled to keep the chief's goats. The chief protests that the loss of these goats will cause his people to go hungry, but the narrator's father, looking triumphant, heartlessly dismisses the chief's concerns (1483). Defeated, humiliated, and angry, Chief Mshlanga declares that the land belongs not to her father but to the chief's people. Then the chief and his son walk away into the bush, never to be seen again.

In this scene the narrator is once again struck by the contrast between the inherent beauty of the African landscape and its inhabitants, on the one hand, and the ugly discord that the Europeans have brought to it: "It was now in the late sunset, the sky a welter of colours, the birds singing their last songs, and the cattle, lowing peacefully, moving past us towards their sheds for the night. It was the hour when Africa is most beautiful; and here was this pathetic, ugly scene, doing no one any good" (1483). Like the previous episode, this one can serve as a basis for helping students identify similar instances of arrogance and brutality in their own "fathers," including the founding fathers and more recent political authorities, in relation to Native Americans, undocumented workers, and people of other nationalities. Teachers might, for example, give students the assignment of researching an episode such as the Trail of Tears or other instances in which the U.S. government took land by force or trickery from the indigenous peoples and then comparing these episodes of the forced removal of Native Americans from their homelands to the removal of Mshlanga's people.

The narrator acquires a third increment of metacognition in the story's final scene, when, about a year later, having learned that the European authorities had given the land on which the chief was living to white settlers and displaced the chief and his people to a reservation 200 miles to the east, returns to the site of the village. This time, the destruction wrought by the Europeans is complete: "There was nothing there. Mounds of red mud, where the huts had been, had long swathes of rotting thatch over them, veined with the red galleries of the white ants. The pumpkin vines rioted everywhere" (1484). In the story's final sentence, the narrator muses ruefully on the utter oblivion—the total lack of self-awareness and metacognition—of the Europeans concerning the now defunct lives and culture of the chief and his people and their own role as the destroyers of those lives and culture: "The settler lucky enough to be allotted the lush warm valley (if he chose to cultivate this particular section) would find, suddenly, in the middle of a mealie field, the plants were growing fifteen feet tall, the weight of the cobs dragging at the stalks, and wonder what unsuspected vein of richness he had struck" (1484), totally oblivious to the fact that this richness—and his—is the result of the impoverishment, destruction, and death that his presence and actions have wrought on the indigenous life.

Here, too, teachers can help students reflect on similar dynamics in American history and present practices. Once again, the treatment of Native Americans is quite similar to that of the native Africans in the story. Students can be helped to identify how European Americans, in both the past and present, are like the European settler the narrator imagines at the end of the story unknowingly benefiting from the impoverishment and destruction of the indigenous people who preceded him. With a little assistance from the teacher, American students can recognize how they and their forebears have profited from the death and destruction of Native Americans, whose past presence on the land inhabited by Americans today is only rarely and dimly realized (when, for example, one finds arrowheads or comes across Indian ruins or burial mounds). Similar points can be made about the residual economic benefits that are intergenerationally transmitted to white people today from the enslavement of Africans and their impoverishment, brutalization, and death, by European Americans. This metacognition can then be extended to include other ways in which Americans today mindlessly and heartlessly profit from the impoverishment of other Others that their schemas have relegated to inferior status.

These passages from the story not only constitute valuable portrayals of the harmful consequences of ethnocentric cognitive schemas, they also offer teachers the opportunity to engage their students in identifying and reflecting on similar cognitive schemas operating in our own culture—and our own minds—today. By helping students trace the causal role of the European cognitive schemas in producing the various kinds of loss and destruction depicted in these scenes, teachers can provide the basis for the development of the students' metacognition concerning their own, similar schemas of Others such as undocumented workers, LGBTQ individuals, Middle Eastern people, and contemporary Africans. Here the behaviors produced by the schemas would often be not the actions of individuals but rather the collective actions constituted by economic and political policies, practices, and institutions.

Metacognition of schema correction

These forms of metacognition—of the nature, origins, faultiness, and harmful consequences of the faulty schemas of self and Other—can also be parlayed into a metacognition of schema change, which will further enable and enhance such change. This metacognition can be fostered by helping students reflect on how they themselves may have been undergoing changes in attitude similar to the narrator's as they have encountered, in the story and in class discussions and investigations of other Others, the kinds of experiences that undermined the girl's ethnocentric schemas and rendered them no longer capable of assimilating or overwriting the reality of the African landscape and its peoples: "slowly," the narrator reports, "that other [European] landscape in my mind faded, and my feet struck directly on the African soil, and I saw the shapes of tree and hill clearly" (1479).

Teachers can use the scene of the girl's encounter with Chief Mshlanga, along with the story's earlier descriptions of more typical encounters between the European settlers and the native Africans, to help students recognize that mere contact with the Other does not guarantee that one will have a fair and accurate perception of the Other—that contact, in fact, can actually work to reinforce their own and their compatriots' faulty schemas of the Other—and to understand the factors that are necessary for them to achieve a fair and accurate perception of the Other. This will enable students to recognize that just because they have some (direct or indirect) contact with a particular type of Other does not mean that they have achieved a fair and accurate perception of the Other, and it will enable them to look for and insist upon the presence of the key factors before assuming that they have anything approaching an adequate understanding.

Teachers may begin the discussion by asking why the encounter with Chief Mshlanga created cognitive dissonance in the girl whereas all her previous, probably daily encounters with Africans had not. Students will point to the chief's status as an obvious factor, and from this observation teachers may introduce research concerning the effects of the Other's status on prejudice reduction, such as a study finding that the higher the status of a white person's black acquaintances, the lower the white person's prejudice and the greater his or her friendly feelings toward black people (Jackman and Crane; qtd. in Schneider 388). From this point teachers might introduce research concerning additional features of contact with the Other that have been found to undermine faulty negative prototypes of the Other—and conversely, what sorts of contact tend to leave the prototypes unchanged or even strengthen them. In addition to the relative status of the group members, stereotype-reducing features of contact include such things as the circumstances, settings, purposes, frequency, and duration of contact and the personalities of the individuals involved.[3] Teachers can then help their students assess the degree to which the various forms of contact that they and Americans in general have with their various Others meet or fail to meet these criteria for effectiveness, thus helping students understand why the mere contact that they and their compatriots may have with the Other does not necessarily lead to accurate perceptions and judgments concerning the Other and may even be counterproductive in this regard. In this discussion, teachers may inform their students, or help them arrive inductively at the recognition, that the key to whether a particular feature of contact facilitates or impedes the correction of faulty prototypes is whether it, in the words of Gordon Allport, "leads to the perception of common interests and common humanity between members of the two groups" (Allport 281). Through discussions and writing assignments, teachers can engage students in examining the ways in which various sorts of contacts they and their compatriots have with Others today either foreground or obscure their sameness with the Other. This metacognition, in turn, will help students avoid assuming that they understand an Other simply because they have some contact with that Other, and it will enable them to monitor the types of contact they have with various Others and orient them toward assessing the validity of their attitudes resulting from this contact on the basis of whether or not the contact produces information of the Other's common interests and humanity.

Candide

Like "The Old Chief Mshlanga," *Candide* too contains significant resources for developing readers' metacognition of their ethnocentrism and its consequences. But its elements work differently than those of

"Mshlanga." First, while Lessing's story focuses on the way ethnocentrism operates on cognition and behavior at the level of the individual, *Candide* emphasizes ethnocentrism's consequences at the collective level. Thus, instead of attending primarily to the consciousness of an individual, Voltaire's readers are led to attend to collective manifestations of ethnocentrism such as classism, religious chauvinism, and nationalism and their violent consequences.

Second, whereas "Mshlanga" promotes metacognition in readers by modeling its development in the narrator-protagonist, *Candide* does so by satirically portraying characters and practices in which such metacognition either is totally lacking or is perverted in ways that produce rather than undermine suffering, oppression, and other forms of injustice. *Candide*, that is, highlights metacognition through its failures, prompting readers to recognize its nature and function and to cultivate it in order to avoid being as ridiculous as the characters and their actions.

Social elitism and classism

This strategy is present from the novel's opening paragraph, where we encounter ethnocentrism in the form of the classism holding sway in Baron Thunder-ten-tronckh's household. The first example of this classism is the refusal of Candide's mother to marry his father because the father could only trace his nobility back seventy-one generations. Teachers can use the patent absurdity of this attitude to help students become aware of, and cast a critical eye on, less severe forms of this same ethnocentrism that they themselves may express, such as when they judge the worthiness (for marriage or friendship) of individuals by the social status of their parents or grandparents.

While the first paragraph exposes the absurdity of classism based on bloodlines, the second ridicules classism that is based on material possessions. Here we are told that the baron was one of the most powerful lords of the region because "his castle had a door and windows" (15). This statement confronts readers with not only the relativism of all wealth, but also the cultural relativism of all standards of wealth, and students will easily recognize how unremarkable, and even primitive, the baron's "castle"—and by extension, the baron's claim to superiority—is by American standards today. From this recognition, teachers can help students become aware of their own (individual and collective) tendency to accord greater respect to people who possess greater wealth. Teachers may introduce empirical studies demonstrating this point and then help students inquire whether their own (current American) assumptions about social status based on wealth might not be as arbitrary and unfounded as those of the baron's time and place.

The arbitrariness of status conveyed by physical appearance and the relativism of standards of beauty—a third form of social elitism—are exposed in the novel's third paragraph, where we are informed that the baroness was greatly admired because she weighed 350 pounds. Since contemporary American culture valorizes thinness and not obesity, the ethnocentrism of the esteem for the obese baroness will be self-evident to American students. Helping students historicize these contrasting standards of beauty can enable them to become cognizant of the relativism and contingency of their own (individual and collective) ideals of beauty. This can be accomplished in various ways. One way is to present images of idealized bodies from different cultures and historical periods and then consider how various material, geographical, social, and historical factors may have contributed to the valorization of the various different sets of ideal bodily features. Such an analysis provides students with a general understanding of the sources as well as the contingency of ideals of physical beauty, which they can then be encouraged to apply to their own notions of beauty.

Candide also promotes metacognition of social elitism by representing the elite as unhappy and as inferior to their subalterns, which motivates readers to divest themselves of elitist aspirations or, at the very least, to understand how elitism can produce or enable unhappiness and lack of virtue. Unhappiness, lack of virtue, or both are evident in most of the endless parade of characters who try to exploit or victimize Candide throughout the novel, as well as in Candide himself during his period of prosperity following his sojourn in El Dorado. Notable exemplars of unhappiness include the Venetian nobleman Pococurante—who, despite immense wealth, power, and learning, is stricken with interminable boredom, able to find pleasure only in having no pleasure, as Candide's companion Martin puts it—and the six deposed monarchs that Candide and Martin encounter at their inn. Exemplars of vice include numerous members of the Parisian elite who cheat Candide or steal from him, various religious authorities who engage in thievery and fornication, and rich merchants and powerful noblemen (including the young baron) who exploit and brutalize Candide along with their slaves.

By asking students to contemplate these exemplars, teachers can help them begin to question aspirations they might harbor to become elite themselves and then, recognizing that power and wealth do not bring happiness, explore what factors do produce fulfillment. Students can come to recognize their own elitist aspirations by recalling childhood, and perhaps current, fantasies about becoming rich and famous and also by reflecting on the insidious idolization of class in America today, as demonstrated by Americans' (including the students' own) fascination with rich and famous people, in the form, for example, of magazines and television shows devoted to the "lifestyles of the rich and famous," as the name of an early television program of this genre phrased it. This metacognition should include awareness of the negative consequences of this idolization, in the form of the growing inequality and class divisions in the United States in the areas of income, wealth, jobs, education, housing, food, security, recreation, and health care. Teachers who wish to have their students develop their metacognition of social elitism further may assign readings or reports on, or simply instruct students about, what social psychologists have called social dominance orientation, a powerful and wide-ranging motive to perceive or establish oneself and one's own group as superior to other groups (see Sidanius and Pratto).

Optimism, the ultimate ethnocentrism

The social elitism (classism) of the Baron's household is immediately shown to be integrally bound up with a much more expansive form of ethnocentrism, which Voltaire names optimism and represents in the absurd and glib pronouncements of the Baron's resident tutor-philosopher, Pangloss. Optimism is a label that refers to Leibnitz's belief that the world we have is the best of all possible worlds, but in *Candide* it also serves as a covert reference to the religious/cosmological ethnocentrism that takes oneself and one's coreligionists to be the primary concern of the universe, the special beneficiaries of the attention and actions of a supreme deity. This ultimate, ontological form of ethnocentrism, expressed in Pangloss's statements that "everything was made for a purpose" and that "all is for the best" (15), manifests itself in the belief that everything that happens is designed to benefit oneself or one's group.

The development of students' metacognition of this ontological ethnocentrism can be initiated by asking them if they can identify any instances of this sort of optimism[4] in American society today. In most classes, students will mention expressions such as the following:

- "Everything happens for a reason."
- "God has a plan for me."
- "God was watching over me."
- "What goes around comes around."
- "Karma."

With some prompting, students can also come to realize that most religions and many instances of patriotism embody one form or another of this sort of ontological optimism, and they can be invited to reflect on which of these religious and secular forms of optimism they themselves and their coreligionists and compatriots may harbor. Many students will recognize, in themselves and others, the belief that their religious group is a "chosen" people, having a privileged position in relation to a divine power and hence in the universe. Many will also hold other, associated ethnocentric beliefs, such as the idea that their religious group is the beneficiary of divine revelation (often in the form of a "holy book" given to the "chosen" people), or the belief that only members of their own religion or sect are "righteous" or will be "saved." American students can recognize secular forms of this ontological ethnocentrism in their own and their compatriots' belief that their country is the greatest in the world, in the doctrine of Manifest Destiny (the belief that Europeans had a divine mandate to take over the continent), and in attitudes such as "My country, right or wrong" and "America: love it or leave it!"

The harmful and unjust consequences of optimism

Then comes the more challenging stage in the development of this form of metacognition: recognizing the ways that such ethnocentric beliefs entail personal and social positions, actions, practices, institutions, and systems that are unjust and harmful. *Candide* offers valuable resources for facilitating this sort of metacognition, in its numerous portrayals of the falsehood and/or the harmful consequences of religious and secular optimism. By helping students carefully examine these instances, teachers can help them recognize the problems entailed by their own similar forms of optimism. It is useful to begin by noting that Voltaire actually titled the novel "Candide, or Optimism," and then asking students why Voltaire might have been so opposed to optimism as to make it the main target of his satire. Then, by directing students' attention to particular passages, teachers can help them recognize that Voltaire opposed optimism for two basic reasons: (1) because there is compelling evidence suggesting that optimism is unfounded, not true, and, more importantly, (2) because optimism is the source of profound suffering and injustice. The falseness of optimism is signaled first in the ridiculousness of its main proponent, Pangloss, and the absurd logic with which he attempts to support it in the face of massive disconfirming evidence. His central argument, presented in the first chapter, consists of three propositions which, though he offers them in pseudo-syllogistic form, have no logical coherence: "'It is demonstrated,' he said, 'that things cannot be otherwise: for, since everything was made for a purpose, everything is necessarily for the best purpose'" (16). His question-begging attempt to exemplify the truth of this claim is even more patently absurd: he claims that the fact that glasses fit on noses and that pants fit over legs demonstrates that noses were made for the purpose of holding up glasses and that legs were made to wear pants (16).

More disturbing than the simple absurdity of Pangloss's philosophical claims are instances in which his (and others') optimism either blithely accepts or actually facilitates preventable human suffering. One example of his idiotic acceptance of unnecessary suffering is his discounting of the rape and disembowelment of Cunegonde by Bulgar soldiers: "But we were well avenged, because the Avars did the same thing to a nearby estate that belonged to a Bulgar lord" (23). A second example is his attitude toward syphilis, which has left him penniless and covered with sores, half-blind, with part of his nose eaten away. When Candide suggests that the source of syphilis must be the devil and not some divine providence, Pangloss rejects this idea with more ludicrous rationalizing, asserting that syphilis "was an indispensable element in the best of worlds, a necessary ingredient, because if Columbus... hadn't caught that disease..., we would now have neither chocolate nor cochineal" (24).

The most damning case against optimism, however, is found in its harmful and often deadly effects. Voltaire signals these effects quite directly in a number of ways. There is, for example, the incident of the orator who preaches charity to a large assembly but then dismisses the starving Candide's plea for assistance when he learns that Candide is not of the same religious persuasion, while his wife, for good measure, empties a chamber pot on Candide's head (21–22). Even more outrageous is the role played by optimism in the death of one of the novel's few admirable characters, James the Anabaptist. When James is thrown overboard after saving a wicked sailor from drowning, Pangloss prevents

Candide from saving James "by proving to him that the Lisbon harbor was formed expressly for the Anabaptist to drown in" (26).

Far more terrible suffering and death are produced by religion and nationalism, the primary institutionalized forms of ontological ethnocentrism. This point is indicated by the brutalization of Candide at the hands of his own military commanders and by the terrible suffering and inhumanity perpetrated by war, both of which are shown to be enabled and even motivated, in part, by ontological ethnocentrism. In the name of honor, glory, and love for the King of the Bulgars (19), Candide is conscripted by two impressment officers and subsequently subjected to merciless beatings by his regiment that "laid bare every muscle and nerve from his neck to his backside," causing him such agony that he "begged them to blow his brains out instead" (20).

Candide indicates further how the religious and nationalist forms of ontological ethnocentrism combine to produce terrible suffering in war. While the opposing kings are praising God for what Voltaire, with bitter irony, describes as "heroic carnage" (20), Candide and the reader are confronted, in graphic honesty that is virtually unheard of in war reporting today, with the horrific consequences of this ethnocentrism:

> Old men with wounds all over their bodies were watching the death throes of butchered women who clutched their children to their bloody breasts; girls who had been disemboweled after satisfying the natural needs several heroes were breathing their last sighs; others, mortally burned, were shrieking for someone to hasten their death. The ground was strewn with brains and severed arms and legs. (21)

A few pages later, Pangloss describes the brutalization suffered by Cunegonde and her family in the same war: "she was disemboweled by Bulgar soldiers after having been raped as much as a woman can be. They smashed the baron's head when he tried to defend her, the baroness was hacked to pieces, and my poor pupil [the baron's son] was treated exactly the same as his sister" (23). Later in the novel, Cunegonde and the Old Woman relate more events of the same sort.

Students can be asked to identify cases in their own nation's history, as well as contemporary instances, in which nationalism and/or religious chauvinism have been implicated in similar human carnage. Examples of more recent history would include the Vietnam War, the Persian Gulf War, and the wars in Iraq and Afghanistan, where innocent civilians were killed by the thousands with napalm, cruise missiles, and drone strikes.

Students may be asked to research (or teachers may simply inform their classes about) the various ethnocentric attitudes and pronouncements that were used to motivate and justify such barbarities. Examples might include the dehumanizing view of Asians held by many Americans during the Vietnam War, as manifested in the belief that "those people"—non-white and non-Christian—didn't value individual human lives to the same extent that "we" Euro-American Christians did and the statement by Air Force general William Boykin during the Iraq war that his Christian god was bigger than the god of an Islamic enemy. With such examples in mind, students may be asked to reflect on their feelings about the horrific results of U.S. military actions and inquire whether their own ontological ethnocentrism might be operating there. One way to expose one's own ethnocentrism is to imagine the tables being turned and then ask oneself, "If they were doing to us what we are doing to them, would I still feel the same way about the action?" If the answer is no, then ethnocentrism is present.

Teachers may also wish to help their students develop metacognition of how various sorts of discrimination, including the benign neglect of certain groups in need, are motivated and justified by nationalism and religious chauvinism. Touchstones in *Candide* for this awareness include the brutalities perpetrated by the Inquisition and the orator's refusal of aid to Candide on religious grounds. Before asking students to reflect on their own personal attitudes and cognitions, it is useful to identify more general, public, anonymous, or institutional forms of religious discrimination in this country. One source of evidence for such discrimination is political surveys, which historically, and also today, indicate that significant numbers of Christian Americans would not vote for a presidential candidate who did not also claim to be Christian. And an even greater number of Americans say they would not vote for a candidate who was agnostic or atheist. Students can be assigned the task of researching these surveys and also statements made by American politicians about their own and others' religious beliefs to see how this form of ethnocentrism permeates the American political atmosphere. And then students can be asked to reflect on the question of whether we, individually and as a nation, are more likely to persecute or neglect the needs of individuals, groups, and nations that do not share our religion. Have they ever, like the orator preaching charity, refused or eschewed helping someone in need because of religious differences? Or because of the other's nationality? Some students may provide testimonials regarding their own attitudes or actions as well as observations about national policies and actions.

The ontological ethnocentrism embodied in nationalism and religion is evident and consequential not only in war but also in colonialism, and *Candide* offers some striking vignettes of colonialism that can be used effectively to promote metacognition of students' own colonialist inclinations and the ontological ethnocentrism that motivates and justifies these impulses. Colonialism is epitomized in the declaration of Cacambo concerning the colonial situation in Paraguay, "The [Jesuits] have everything, the people nothing" (49), and the concrete reality of this domination is portrayed a few paragraphs later when we encounter the Jesuit commander entering "a shady retreat adorned with a pretty colonnade of green and gold marble, and trelliswork cages enclosing parrots, colibris, hummingbirds, guinea fowl and all sorts of other rare birds," preparing to consume "an excellent meal... served in golden vessels,... while the Paraguayans were eating corn from wooden bowls in the blazing sunlight of the open fields" (50).

The terrible human costs of ethnocentrism in the form of colonialism are made even more explicit by the old man in Eldorado who tells Candide and Cacambo that it is only the geographical inaccessibility of Eldorado that has saved it from the rapacity of the Europeans, who, he says, "would kill every one of us to get [our gold and precious stones]" (62). The brutality of colonializing ethnocentrism is further demonstrated when, after leaving Eldorado, Candide and Cacambo come across a black man who is missing a hand and a leg. They learn that the man is the slave of a wealthy Dutch merchant who had his hand cut off because he got his finger caught under a millstone in the sugar mill where he worked and his leg amputated because he tried to run away. "That's the price of the sugar you eat in Europe," he tells Candide and Cacambo (68).

Primed with these examples of the brutalities of colonialist ethnocentrism, students can be asked to identify historical and contemporary instances of American colonialism and to research its human costs. Teachers may begin by asking if the students think the old Eldorado man's characterization of Europeans and Voltaire's example of the double amputee have any historical accuracy or if instead they are simply examples of the sort of exaggeration for effect that one finds throughout *Candide*. Discussion or research on this question can bring to light actual historical instances of such brutality. One of the most striking and relevant to American students is the treatment that the Arawak Indians of the Bahamas received at the hands of Columbus. From the first five pages of Howard Zinn's *A People's History of the United States*, students can learn that although the Arawaks greeted Columbus and his men with hospitality and generosity, Columbus returned the favor by enslaving them and demanding that they each bring him a monthly quota of gold. Those who failed to do so "had their hands cut off and bled to death" (4). A priest who accompanied Columbus on his second voyage wrote that Columbus's men "thought nothing of knifing Indians by tens and twenties and of cutting slices off them to test the sharpness of their blades" (qtd. in Zinn 6). The role played by religion in Columbus's horrific ethnocentrism is quite evident from his own testimony. "He was full of religious talk," Zinn writes (3), declaring, for example, "Let us in the name of the Holy Trinity go on sending all the slaves that can be sold" (qtd. in Zinn 4). And he viewed the opportunity to enslave the Arawaks and steal their gold as a gift from God: "Thus the eternal God, our Lord, gives victory to those who follow His way over apparent impossibilities" (qtd. in Zinn 3). Such historical facts can help American students recognize both the terrible costs that ontological ethnocentrism can exact and the degree to which their own nation is thoroughly implicated, from its origins, in such ethnocentrism and its atrocities.

There may be greater resistance on the part of some students to acknowledging their own contemporary and personal ethnocentrism and its injustices. But many will have some knowledge of the ways in which they, as consumers of food, clothing, electronics, and automobiles, are themselves implicated in colonialist ethnocentrism, and this knowledge can be used as a starting point for them to ponder or research the human costs of the sugar and other products that they and their compatriots consume today. Many students will have some awareness of the labor and living conditions under which their shirts, cell phones, and fruit are produced. Elaborating and concretizing these conditions through discussion and research can provide the basis for them to explore their thoughts and feelings concerning what responsibility they themselves, individually and collectively, may have for the human suffering and injustice resulting from these economic arrangements. And more specifically, they can be asked to explore whether they experience the same degree of concern for the plights of the Asian or Central or South American workers that they would if their own compatriots or family members were subjected to these conditions. If the answer is no (as it will most often be), then the question follows: is ethnocentrism a reason? That is, is the humanity, or the suffering, or the deservingness of the ethnic Other somehow perceived as less than one's own or that of one's family? Are Americans and/or Christians more deserving of comfort, security, longevity, and happiness than people who are not Christian and/or who live on the other side of the globe? To the degree that students can recognize and own such ethnocentric impulses, they may experience a cognitive dissonance that will motivate them to alter their ethnocentric thinking and actions regarding the Other.

Religious ethnocentrism

The most difficult form of metacognition for many students will be that regarding their own religious beliefs. Many will feel, as Columbus did, that their religion is the one true religion, and that as adherents to the true religion, they have a privileged relationship not only to a providential deity but also to the truth—one that need not rely on evidence or be subjected to any sort of critical examination. But since religion is so often implicated in the most harmful instances of ethnocentrism, developing metacognition concerning one's own religious beliefs and practices is a crucial—and perhaps even indispensable—component of cosmopolitan education. *Candide* provides a basis for developing such a metacognition. It does so in the form of a critique of religion that can help such students begin to recognize the degree to which their own religious convictions are the result not simply of some supposed direct pipeline they have to the truth but rather of their particular geographical, historical, cultural, and familial circumstances and upbringing.

A key scene for initiating this sort of metacognition is the encounter of Candide and Cacambo with the cannibalistic Oreillons. The episode begins when Candide kills two monkeys he observes chasing and biting the buttocks of two girls, only to be told by Cacambo that the monkeys are actually the girls' lovers. Candide is incredulous, but Cacambo schools him in the principle of cultural relativism: this, he says is an example of "how people behave when they've been given a different upbringing" (56). A similar principle applies to the cannibalism of the Oreillons, who subsequently take the two men captive at the behest of the girls and prepare to eat them. In the case of the Oreillons, however, the cultural difference (cannibalism) is itself traced back to differences in material circumstances. While Candide condemns their cannibalism as "inhuman" and "unchristian," the more cosmopolitan and pragmatic

Cacambo recognizes it as a function of their particular material circumstances. Everybody kills their enemies, he says, and if Christian Europeans don't also eat them, it's because they have other things to eat. "But you don't have the same resources as we do," he tells the Oreillons, "and it's certainly better to eat your enemies than to abandon the fruit of your victory to crows and ravens" (57).

Here teachers can kick start students' metacognition through a kind of shock recognition. Most students will side with Candide in condemning cannibalism and will in fact view it as one of the most primitive, savage, and inhuman acts that humans are capable of. But teachers can state that many Americans and Europeans, including some of the students themselves, are self-professed cannibals and, in fact, consider their cannibalism to be an essential part of their religious practice. Most students will respond to such an assertion with an incredulity greater than Candide's, but a few will connect the teacher's statement with the Catholic doctrine of transubstantiation, which holds that when the priest blesses the bread and wine during the sacrament of communion, those substances are magically transformed into the literal blood and body of Christ, such that those who partake of the communion are literally eating Jesus' body and drinking his blood. (Protestant doctrine, it may be noted, holds that the bread and wine merely *symbolize* Jesus' body and blood.) Following the initial shock of this revelation, students can be helped to recognize the ethnocentrism operating beneath their bifurcated view of cannibalism: their horror at the Other's cannibalism, coexisting with their placid acceptance, respect, or even veneration of their own or their compatriots' cannibalistic practices is a striking example of how we often see our own actions very differently from the way we see these same actions when they are engaged in by the Other.

Further metacognition concerning the ethnocentrism of students' religious beliefs and practices can be facilitated by asking them to reflect, in class discussions and/or in writing assignments, on the similarities and differences among the beliefs and practices of the victims of the shipwreck, the Inquisitors, the Eldoradoans, Martin, the dervish, and themselves, and also to consider the reasons for these similarities and differences—thus helping the students achieve metacognition not only of what they believe but also of the material, geographical, social, cultural, and psychological factors that have played a formative role in the development of their beliefs. Through reflection and discussion, students will be able to identify significant differences among these characters in their religious practices and in their ideas about the existence and nature of gods and these gods' relation to humans.

The people praying on the sinking ship obviously believe that there is a god who could save their lives but also that he might not do so in the absence of their petition. This view of the deity will be quite familiar to most students, since it will be very similar to their own. The theism of the inquisitors who conduct the auto-da-fé will prove, on close examination, a bit less familiar and somewhat troubling. They, too, clearly believe that there is a divine power that can and will intervene in natural events to help humans, but they also evidently assume that something more than prayer is needed to persuade the deity to do so—something similar to the human sacrifices practiced by more ancient and "primitive" religions. On this view, god is not simply a benign presence but rather, like the Old Testament Yahweh, a jealous and vengeful god who must be propitiated with gifts, including human lives. Some students may point out that a similar divine figure is implied in the Christian doctrine of the crucifixion. The contradiction between such divine actions and qualities and the common assumption that "god is love" will ignite a cognitive dissonance in some students that can spur the development of further metacognition.

The god of the Eldoradoans will be the most comfortable one for many students, but the contrast between the Eldoradoans' religious practices and the students' own may produce further cognitive dissonance. The god of the Eldoradoans is the all-knowing, all-loving, munificent power that may students have been taught to believe in, but the Eldoradoans' religious institutions and practices are strikingly unlike those of Christianity and most other major religions—most notably in the fact that they "have no monks who teach, argue, rule, plot, and burn people who don't agree with them" (63) and that they do not ask their god for anything but rather "constantly thank him" (63). The fact that the Eldoradoans' practices are consistent with their belief in a purely benign deity while the practices of many students' religions will not be can produce a dissonance that results in alterations of their beliefs or practices or both.

Martin's fatalistic, pessimistic Manichean beliefs and the dervish's cynical deism will be not only unfamiliar to many students but actually quite threatening to some. The strangeness of these characters' beliefs constitutes an excellent opportunity to help students reflect on why these characters—or anyone—would believe what they believe. And their reflection on this question not only constitutes valuable training in taking the perspective of the Other, it can also be a stepping stone to inquiring why they themselves have the religious beliefs they do. Martin believes that the god that supposedly created the world has abandoned it to some malevolent being (73), and while the dervish doesn't posit that this god has been superseded by a devil, he does share Martin's conviction that this god cares not one whit for human beings.

These beliefs of Martin and the dervish constitute a radical assault on religious ethnocentrism—the belief that one's own group has a privileged position in the universe vis-à-vis other groups—for they reject the anthropocentrism, the position that humans have a privileged status vis-à-vis other forms of life and matter, that forms its foundation. (The importance of anthropocentrism to the ontological ethnocentrism of religion can be seen in the virulence and brutality with which the Catholic church persecuted Copernicus and Galileo for contesting the dogma that the earth was the center of the universe.) And some students will experience these beliefs as a threat to their core sense of self for the same reason. It can be useful to help students recognize and acknowledge the fear and also anger they may feel in response to these deist-Manichean beliefs and become cognizant of why they find these beliefs so threatening.

Then teachers can pose the question of why, if these beliefs are threatening, anyone would subscribe to them. Here the text provides a compelling answer in the form of Martin's explanation to Candide of why he is a Manichean. The reason he doesn't subscribe to the optimistic belief that the world is under the control of a benign power, Martin says, is because he can't: "I can't think otherwise" (73). The reality of the human condition makes it impossible for him to hold such a belief. And in emphasizing that Martin has a much more extensive experience of the world than most people ("I've seen and experienced so much that I'm a Manichean," 73) and that he is given to thought and reflection (he is described as a scholar, 71), the text suggests that his position has greater evidentiary support than the other beliefs represented here. His credibility is further indicated by his name and his declaration, "I can't think otherwise," which recall Martin Luther and his famous refusal to recant his denunciation of certain church doctrines with the declaration, "Ich kann nicht anderes" ("I can't [think, believe, or do] otherwise"). Similarly, by describing the dervish as "the best philosopher in Turkey" (111), the text accords an equally high degree of credibility to his belief that whatever power might be in control of the world cares no more about the welfare of humans than a rich merchant cares about whether the mice on his ships are comfortable (111). The fact that the dervish is cynical and unhappy indicates that he is not pleased with his belief but rather, like Martin, sees no other credible conclusion.

The refutation of ontological ethnocentrism

This appears to be the position of the text itself: ontological ethnocentrism is so untenable in light of the massive human suffering that exists, the novel suggests, that even its most ardent proponents don't really believe it. Voltaire makes this point by having Candide, when asked what optimism is, reply, "It's a mania for insisting that everything is all right when everything is going wrong" (69) and by having Pangloss himself admit, in the novel's final pages, that he no longer believes his own doctrine (110).

Candide also signals the untenability of ontological ethnocentrism in other ways, most notably by the fact that the world is rife with suffering and injustice and that members of self-designated chosen groups are no more immune to human suffering than are their supposedly less important ethnic Others, as well as by the fact that the efforts of the chosen ones to elicit succor from their supposed divine benefactor come to naught. This point is made quite dramatically when everyone except Pangloss, Candide, and a "brutal sailor" perish in the Lisbon shipwreck, including all the passengers who were praying for deliverance (26). The absence of divine intervention is also underscored by the results of the auto-da-fé that is performed in order to elicit divine prevention of another earthquake. In direct contradiction of the assumption that burning, hanging, and flogging several supposed heretics "was an infallible means of preventing the earth from quaking" (28), readers are informed that "that same day the earth shook again, with a terrible uproar" (29).

Similarly, when the ship of the Dutch captain who stole from Candide sinks and Candide declares to Martin that this event is evidence of cosmic justice and divine intervention, his optimistic claim is abruptly refuted by Martin's rejoinder: "What about the passengers?" (74). Recognition of the falseness of one's own ontological ethnocentrism can be facilitated by reflecting on a similar common sentiment that is inevitably uttered by one or more survivors of a disaster in which others have perished: the conviction that they survived "because God was watching out for me." The critical response here is, "What about all the people who didn't survive? Does God not care about them? Does God only care about you?" The absurdity of this ontological ethnocentrism is quite patent in cases where two groups are praying for opposite results. Voltaire stages this absurdity at the beginning of chapter III, with two kings simultaneously thanking God for helping them slaughter tens of thousands of the other's troops. This episode is simply a synecdoche for a ubiquitous phenomenon: opposing groups, including religions, each claiming inherent, and sometimes even cosmic, superiority over the other.

Students will be able to recognize similar examples of dueling ontological ethnocentrisms not only in the Crusades but also in the 9/11 attacks and in George W. Bush's "crusade" (the word he first used, before being censored by his handlers) in response to the attacks. And they will also be able to recognize less disastrous but more frequent examples of the same attitude in the prayers of athletes for success or victory and in these same athletes' frequent attribution of success or victory to divine intervention. Reflecting on such episodes can induce cognitive dissonance in readers who subscribe to some form of ontological ethnocentrism, and teachers can ask students to identify similar contemporary events that might challenge their own ontological ethnocentrism.

Students can also be helped to critique arguments that they and their fellows may offer in support of their ontological ethnocentrism. Most notable are anecdotes in which students believe their prayers to have been answered or instances of disaster that were averted, often, in the minds of students, "because God was watching out for me." In response to such supposed evidence in support of their ontological ethnocentrism, students can be asked to identify instances where their prayers were not answered or disasters, for themselves or other innocents, that were not averted.

Candide's refutation of optimism raises the question of why so many people subscribe to some form of ontological ethnocentrism. What are the causes of such religious views? If the optimistic religious positions aren't supported by evidence, why do so many people hold to them so tenaciously? This question becomes the basis of developing metacognition of one's own religious beliefs.

In nurturing students' metacognition concerning their investment in their religious beliefs, teachers can begin by asking, "What factors besides evidence play a role in determining what a person believes?" If ideas are not forthcoming from students, teachers can pursue the issue by inquiring, "Why does Candide subscribe to Pangloss's optimistic worldview?" "Why are different religions dominant in different regions of the world—such as Christianity in Europe and the Americas, Islam in the Middle East, Hinduism in India, and so on?" From such questions, students can come to recognize that one major reason most people believe what they do is because those are the beliefs into which they have been socialized—one might even say brainwashed—from birth by their families and/or cultures. The fact that the great majority of people on the planet, historically and today, share the beliefs of their family and/or larger culture indicates that socialization is a major determinant of people's religious beliefs, including probably the students' own. Teachers can help students recognize this fact about themselves as well, by asking, "If you had been born in a different country, with parents and an entire culture who had a different religion, would you believe what you believe now?" Most students will acknowledge that if they had been born into a different religion, they would probably have those beliefs rather than those they currently hold. With a little further reflection and some introspection, some students may come to realize that indoctrination, rather than evidence or reason, has been the dominant factor in determining their beliefs, and that they are in a very real way captive to the accident of their birth. And this realization, in turn, can motivate them to examine their beliefs more critically in relation to whatever evidence might bear upon the question of their validity.

Psychological needs and biases are two additional prominent determinants of religious belief. Teachers can help students recognize the role played by such psychological factors by asking them to reflect on why Pangloss—and to a lesser extent Candide—clings so tenaciously to his belief that all is well when he is surrounded by evidence to the contrary. Many students will recognize that he does so because of the profound security that this belief provides him. Students may then be asked to identify various beliefs concerning a providential deity that they and/or their compatriots hold that provide a sense of security for them. The most reassuring beliefs will usually be the guarantee of immortality to the faithful and a more general promise of justice: the good will ultimately be rewarded (and the wicked punished)—two beliefs that can reduce anxiety about death and other catastrophes to which humans are vulnerable.

Teachers may help students develop their metacognition of this psychological function of beliefs by asking them to research and report on—or by simply informing them of—various classical and contemporary accounts of this function. For example, teachers can recall Marx's famous statement that "religion is the opium of the masses" and ask students to explain what that means: namely, that religion reduces the pain of living by dulling awareness, putting people to sleep, metaphorically speaking. They might also introduce Freud's notion that the belief in an omnipotent, omniscient deity is the product of an infantile wish for a strong, protective father-figure. Bringing in more contemporary, empirically based formulations of the religion-as-security-blanket explanation will likely be even more effective in helping students explore the psychological needs that may be informing their own beliefs and those of their coreligionists. Two such formulations can be found in Belief in a Just World Theory and Terror Management Theory.

Belief in a Just World (BJW) is a version of Panglossian optimism (see Lerner 151). It involves the conviction that people who are good and do good will prosper and that people who are bad and do bad things will suffer. Individuals and cultures vary greatly in the degree to which they subscribe to this belief, and it is strongest in individuals who believe "in the presence of an omniscient, omnipotent force, that sees to it that justice and goodness triumphs, and that wickedness is punished" (Lerner 142). Such individuals, like Pangloss, will often resort to various kinds of cognitive distortions (psychological defense mechanisms) in order to maintain their belief. For example, high BJW people often rationalize their own misfortunes, as Pangloss did his syphilis, as producing a net gain in their lives. A study of individuals who had been crippled for life found that the great majority of them had concluded, like Pangloss, "that it is all for the best, that they are following God's plan" (Lerner 163). More significantly and harmfully, in order to maintain their belief in a just world, high BJW individuals tend to ignore or discount the suffering of innocent victims of misfortune—as Pangloss did with the drowning James—and, in many cases, even blame them for their suffering (Maes 9; Lerner 20ff.) Indeed, a series of studies found that "the more unjust a situation appeared, the greater the devaluation of the innocent victim involved" (Maes 10). A 1971 study of responses to the "victims" of the draft lottery found, for example, that while most of the young men subjected to the lottery responded with sympathy and liking to the unlucky "losers" of the lottery, high BJW individuals tended to view the random outcomes of the lottery as somehow deserved (Maes 10) and responded with resentment and rejection to the unlucky individuals who would now inevitably be drafted and probably sent to Vietnam (Lerner 140; Maes

10). More significant for cosmopolitanism, another study found that high BJW individuals tended to blame "economically deprived people in the third world" for their plight (Montada and Lerner, "Overview" 3).

Belief in a Just World is a fundamental and probably even universal human inclination (Lerner 12–15) that allows people to cope with the anxieties of human existence: "People want to and have to believe they live in a just world so that they can go about their daily lives with a sense of trust, hope, and confidence in their future" (Lerner 14). Lerner concludes "that the desire to see justice done in one's environment is sufficient to elicit justice-restoring cognitive distortion among a *substantial portion* of reasonably bright, well-educated young adults" (Lerner 158).

But such individuals pay a price for their cognitive distortions, and they also exact a cost from the rest of us. It is thus desirable to help high BJW individuals reduce the intensity of their belief so as to reduce the cognitive distortions—and hence the harm—that it causes. One way to do so is through the development of metacognition concerning this belief. As Montada and Lerner observe, "There are good reasons to believe that BJW as a fundamental belief gains its strongest impact at the intuitive emotional level of functioning. The more rational reflection is induced, the less the impact of BJW on the person's reaction" (Montada and Lerner, "Preface" viii). By developing metacognition concerning whatever degree of belief in a just world they may harbor, students can arm themselves against the automatic operation of this belief and thus reduce the harmful—and, ironically, often unjust—cognitive distortions that it produces. And learning about BJW theory and research can form the basis of such metacognition.

An even more effective way to develop students' metacognition is to administer all or part of the questionnaire that is used to measure BJW as a way of providing them with knowledge of how their degree of BJW compares with that of other students in the class. Examples of questions, with which individuals indicate agreement on a scale of 1–6, include (Lerner 139):

- Basically, the world is a just place.
- By and large, people deserve what they get.
- Many people suffer through no fault of their own (reverse scored).
- People who get "lucky breaks" have usually earned their good fortune.
- People who meet with misfortune often have brought it on themselves.

Comparing their individual scores on this measure with the class average can help students become more cognizant of key assumptions of theirs that may influence their perceptions and judgments of various Others. At the same time, teachers should inform students that research has found that even individuals who express very little agreement with these propositions may harbor preconscious "primitive," irrational BJW scripts such as "bad things happen to bad people" that can, under certain conditions, lead them to discount or derogate innocent victims at home and abroad, even when they consciously know better (see Lerner, "Two Forms" 251ff.). Such actions are the result of "the automatic application of very simple causal schemas, or scripts that initially appeared very early in their lives and persist throughout adulthood—bad outcomes are caused by bad people" (Lerner, "Two Forms" 255). These preconscious cognitive scripts and the processes of perception and judgment that they enact are not available to introspection (Lerner, "Two Forms" 258). They can only be inferred by their outcomes—such as ignoring another's suffering or viewing it as deserved—which means that students need to be skeptical of all perceptions and judgments of this sort, and take extra time and effort in such instances to perceive the other fairly and accurately. Teachers can help students develop metacognition of these preconscious cognitive process—and also help them establish a meta-script of extra care in response to such judgments—by explaining the operation of preconscious scripts and assigning students the task of finding manifestations of their operations in their own emotional reactions to people in need, in the utterances of political figures, and in the reactions of literary characters, such as Pangloss, Cunegonde, and the Old Woman.

Terror Management Theory (TMT) is another research paradigm that has demonstrated the security-providing function of ethnocentrism in general and religion in particular. "Terror management is an ongoing process that people continually pursue to ward off the potential for anxiety that results from the knowledge that death is inevitable" (Pyszczynski et al. "Dual-Process" 841).

TMT has found that when individuals are reminded, even subliminally, of their mortality, they respond by clinging more tenaciously to their religious beliefs and worldviews, according greater value to others who share their beliefs, and proselytizing, derogating, and even aggressing against those who hold different beliefs (Pyszczynski et al. "Why"). Such efforts to maintain and advance one's worldview, TMT researchers argue, serves to "defend against death by enabling the individual to construe himself or herself as a valuable participant in a meaningful universe" (Pyszczynski et al. "Dual-Process" 835). And of course religious beliefs that promise immortality to the faithful provide the most powerful defenses against death anxiety.

After becoming familiar with TMT, students may be asked to reflect, in discussion or in a writing assignment, on their feelings about their own mortality, on their beliefs about death, and on the comfort they receive from their religion or worldview. Teachers may initiate the process by asking students what emotional comforts or other psychological benefits are provided by the belief in a providential deity. Most students will readily recognize that protection against death anxiety is a major benefit of such beliefs, and through discussion, they can become aware of how these beliefs can also help people defend against other aspects of human finitude, including lack of knowledge and power, and provide a basis for hope in even the bleakest of situations. Awareness of these general benefits can then lead to an understanding of the fact that people often strongly, and even violently, resist any information or other people who challenge these beliefs.[5]

This general understanding, in turn, provides a basis for students to develop metacognition of their own ego-protective, or defensive, uses of ontological ethnocentrism. Such metacognition can be fostered by engaging students in reflection and discussion of questions such as the following:

▶ Do you believe that life after death is possible and that you will continue to exist after you die?
▶ If so, what form do you imagine that life to take? Is the life after death literal or metaphorical? That is, do you believe that you personally will continue to exist and be conscious, or do you view immortality as taking the form of living on in your descendants, in other people's memories of you (e.g., in fame), or in the enduring impact that your life and actions will have after your death?
▶ How would you feel if you were to be convinced that your belief in life after death was not true? For example, what if you were to realize that there is no such thing as personal immortality? Would you feel anxious? Afraid? Depressed? Angry?
▶ What if you were to realize that your entire culture and its worldview will sooner or later fade from existence, erasing all your contributions to it? How would you feel? What might you do?

In addition to engaging students in reflecting on their emotional investments in their beliefs about death, teachers can also promote more general metacognition about ethnocentric beliefs by having their students grapple with questions such as the following:

- How do you feel when someone challenges or questions your beliefs, values, or way of life? Anxious? Angry? Contemptuous?
- How do you feel when you simply encounter beliefs contrary to your own, such as those of another religion or agnosticism or atheism?
- Did you feel any discomfort, anxiety, anger, or disdain when reading or discussing any of the beliefs in *Candide*, such as those of Martin or the dervish?
- Do you feel any discomfort now, while discussing the question of why you believe what you do?

Metacognition concerning theistic beliefs can also be promoted by familiarizing students with the perspective of evolutionary psychology concerning belief in god. Evolutionary psychology argues that people believe in a divine providence because the process of natural selection has hardwired the human brain to maximize survival by responding in certain ways to important events and features of the natural world and the social world, and that such religious beliefs are simply a byproduct of these hardwired brain mechanisms. The key mechanism is what has been called our "hypersensitive agency detection device (HADD)" (Barrett), our tendency to attribute the causes of events to the actions of intentional agents (human, superhuman, or animal). This HADD emerged in humans, according to evolutionary psychology, because of its survival value. Attributing a rustling of leaves, for example, to the movement of an enemy or a predator could save one's life, whereas failing to do so could be fatal. If one is wrong in such an attribution, and the rustling was actually caused by the wind or a falling acorn rather than a living agent (a false positive), no harm generally results. If one mistakenly makes the opposite inference, however, and attributes the cause to the wind when it is actually a hungry bear (a false negative), the consequences could be disastrous. Thus, as one evolutionary psychologist explains, "Our HADD...prompts us to find agency among ambiguous information around us. We eagerly search and often find evidence of agents acting around us. Such a tendency warmly receives the idea of gods and makes belief in gods very natural" (Barrett 90; see also Atran). This sort of metacognition concerning one's belief in a divine providence can function much like the knowledge that humans in general have a genetically based proclivity for sweet and fatty foods: it can alert one to the need to intercept and resist a genetically based tendency that has been found to be counterproductive to human well-being in the world today.

Finally, students' metacognition of their ethnocentric religious beliefs can be enhanced by asking them to assess the evidence concerning (a) the validity and (b) the consequences, especially the harmful ones, of their beliefs. To help students reflect on the consequences of their beliefs, it can be useful to familiarize them, through assigned readings or reports, with scholarship on how the major religions have been implicated in violence and indifference to human suffering, including war, persecution, and genocide of the sorts represented in *Candide*. Useful books include Charles Selengut's *Sacred Fury: Understanding Religious Violence*, Regina Schwartz's *The Curse of Cain: The Violent Legacy of Monotheism*, Hector Avalos's *Fighting Words: The Origins of Religious Violence*, James Wellman's *Belief and Bloodshed: Religion and Violence across Time and Tradition*, and Mark Juergensmeyer's *Terror in the Mind of God: The Global Rise of Religious Violence*. Students may be asked to identify additional, more recent examples. Harris and Hitchens can help here as well. Most classes will be able to recognize Southern Protestant preachers' support of American slavery and segregation before and after the Civil War, the Catholic church's acquiescence in the Holocaust, the attacks of 9/11, and the Catholic church's self-serving responses to child rape by its priests as instances.

Reflecting on the validity of their beliefs will be harder for many students than acknowledging the negative effects of their religion, for two reasons. First, because of our theocentric culture, many—perhaps most—American students will not be conversant with arguments refuting theism. To help overcome this problem, teachers may wish to have their classes read or hear reports on the arguments put forth by books refuting theism, such as Sam Harris's *The End of Faith* or *Letter to a Christian Nation*, Christopher Hitchens's *God Is Not Great: How Religion Poisons Everything*, Hitchens's collection *The Portable Atheist: Essential Readings for the Nonbeliever*, Richard Dawkins's *The God Delusion*, and Daniel Dennett's *Breaking the Spell: Religion as a Natural Phenomenon*.

Second, to the extent that their sense of self is integrally bound up with their religion, it will be difficult for students to think thoughts or consider evidence that undermine their beliefs (see Alcorn). Thinking these thoughts can be made less threatening by helping students encounter or imagine other people thinking them, and then evaluating their validity. *Candide* provides various opportunities for doing this, most notably in response to Martin's position and comments. But the most severe and direct challenge to theism in this text is that put forth by the "famous dervish ... known as the best philosopher in Turkey" (111), who categorically rejects any sort of belief in a providential deity, declaring that the welfare of humans matters not at all to whatever power might be responsible for their creation. Students may be asked to discuss what evidence there is to support or to contradict the dervish's declaration.

The novel's ending, Candide's proclamation, "We must cultivate our garden" (113), also constitutes a powerful if more implicit rejection of the optimistic, ethno- and anthropo-centric belief in a providential deity. To help students recognize the eschewal here of any reliance on a providential deity, and the suggestion of an alternative strategy for finding some meaning and contentment in life, teachers can ask students to consider the weight of each word of Candide's statement. Why, for example, did Voltaire choose the word "garden" instead of "farm"? Perceptive students will point out that "garden" alludes to the Garden of Eden, which Pangloss mentions half a page earlier, and that Voltaire may therefore want his readers to compare and contrast the life of Adam and Eve in the Garden of Eden with the life of Candide and his friends on their farm. Students will recognize a stark difference between the two: in the (prelapsarian) Garden of Eden, a quintessential providential deity provided everything necessary for Adam and Eve to lead a life of continuous bliss, whereas no such power is providing for Candide and his friends.

Metacognition of altruistic impulses

At the same time, however, referring to their farm as a garden may suggest that a modicum of contentment may not be beyond their reach. More specifically, by discussing Voltaire's selection of the words "must," "we/our," and "cultivate," students can see the text suggesting that the best chance at happiness is for humans to recognize necessity ("must"), including the various forms of their human finitude, and then work together, collectively ("we," "our"), within these limits to alter the natural world ("cultivate"), including humans themselves, to the extent possible to maximize human well-being. The word "cultivate" is especially meaningful here, since it shares its root with "agriculture" and "culture," the former referring to what is perhaps the most important and fundamental way humans have altered the natural world to sustain their life, and the latter designating the way humans alter their own nature. Candide's—and Voltaire's—final words can thus be read as stating that while we can't realistically sit back and wait for happiness to shower down on us from the heavens, we can, by working together to transform the physical world and ourselves, have a chance at a life that is bearable and perhaps even fulfilling.

The paragraphs preceding these concluding words provide additional suggestions about this strategy and can be used to help students develop metacognition not of their various ethnocentric impulses but rather of opposite, cooperative and altruistic impulses in themselves that constitute the ethical core of cosmopolitanism. The novel here invites readers to reflect on what factors are necessary for contentment and happiness. Candide and his friends, returning from their visit to the dervish, encounter "a kindly-looking old man sitting in front of his door beneath an arbor of orange trees, enjoying the fresh air" (112). Candide and his companions learn that the man and his children have twenty acres, which they cultivate. "Our work," the man tells them, "keeps us free of three great evils: boredom, vice, and poverty" (112). Observing that this man's life is better than that of the kings he has met, Candide resolves, "we must cultivate our garden" (113), and in the final paragraphs, Candide and friends, bereft of whatever youth, beauty, wealth, and power they once possessed, manage to achieve a modicum of contentment when they enact what the novel calls the "commendable plan" of "work[ing] without theorizing."

The novel's brief description of this work can be used to help students develop metacognition of their own productive and altruistic impulses, which are the key motives underwriting cosmopolitanism.[6] By asking students what it is about these characters' work that makes their lives satisfying, teachers can help them recognize three features that are crucial to whatever satisfaction work can provide. First, each individual's job is something he is good at: "each began to exercise his own talents" (113). Second, the work is consequential, productive: "The little farm yielded abundant crops" (113). And third, the work benefits others, providing a service or commodity that they need or enjoy: "Everyone made himself useful" (113). Having identified these three factors of satisfying work, students can then be asked to reflect on their own experiences of working to see if they too find gratification in these features. Of particular importance here is the satisfaction one gets from making or doing something that benefits others. By recognizing, and understanding the significance of, such experiences, students will enhance the role of this altruistic impulse in the positions and actions they take, including those concerning distant Others.

Teachers may then help students explore why these three features of work are satisfying. Here, Marx's notion of alienated labor and Erik Erikson's concept of generativity can be useful. These two concepts recognize that maintaining an identity—a sense of oneself as a force that matters in the world—is the most fundamental human motivation, and that doing work that one can see benefiting other people is the best way to maintain such a sense of self.[7] For Marx, a fundamental human need is to transform the material world into objects that other people need and use. When we do so, and see other people using our products, we get a sense of our own productivity and creativity reflected back to us from their use. Capitalism, in Marx's view, interferes with this crucial identity support, by preventing wage laborers from exercising their unique talents and abilities (alienation from their activity), preventing them from making the products they would choose (alienation from their products), pitting them against each other in competition for jobs (alienation from other people), and preventing them from expressing their essential human nature of creativity (alienation from their species-being).

Erikson conceptualized this human need to be of use to others in somewhat broader and less explicitly materialist terms. Adult humans, he maintained, are "so constituted as to *need to be needed*" (130; emphasis in original). He named this impulse generativity, which he described as "the instinctual power behind various forms of selfless 'caring'" (131). This generativity, or "need to be needed" (132), manifests itself most fully not in a Marxian need for unalienated labor but rather in the need to teach: "we are the teaching species," Erikson declared, adding that "the teaching passion is not restricted to the teaching profession" (130–131).

Generativity, Erikson indicates further, is a kind of instinctual impulse that can constitute the core of a new, universalist ethic, one that entails cosmopolitanism and a quest for global justice. "There may be resources for peace even in our 'animal nature,'" he states, "if we will only learn to nurture our nature" (230). The basis of this ethic is universal generativity: the acknowledgment of "the responsibility of each individual for the potentialities of all generations and of all generations for each individual" (157). It is characterized by "a universal sense of generative responsibility toward all human beings" (131) that "makes every child conceived a subject of universal responsibility" (238). And in this view, helping others achieve fulfillment is the best way to attain fulfillment for oneself (see 231–234).

Helping students become aware of their own—and the general human—need to be needed as an alternative to competition, superiority, and domination is critical to enhancing their likelihood of engaging in such actions generally and of enacting cosmopolitanism more specifically. Most Americans tend toward the assumption, which constitutes the core of classical economic theory, that humans are motivated primarily if not exclusively by narrow self-interest and the cold calculations and competitive actions that it entails. In this view, any cooperation they engage in must be purely tactical or strategic, a means to the end of self-promotion (see Bracher, *Literature*, chapter 4). As Dale T. Miller and Melvin Lerner have pointed out, this assumption blocks people's awareness of their own altruistic and cosmopolitan inclinations and potentialities, and this blindness, in turn, prevents or significantly reduces their acting on these impulses and developing the potential for them to overcome the impulses of narrow self-interest. "The theory of self-interest," Miller observes, "has spawned a norm of self-interest, the consequence of which is that people often act and speak in accordance with their perceived self-interest solely because they believe to do otherwise is to violate a powerful descriptive and prescriptive expectation" (1053). Miller explains two ways in which "the ideology of self-interest ... functions as a powerful self-fulfilling force":

> First, individualistic cultures structure their social institutions to reflect their belief that people are naturally disposed to pursue their self-interest, which results in these institutions fostering the very behavior their structure presupposes occurs naturally.... Second,... individualistic cultures spawn social norms that induce people to follow their material self-interest rather than their principles or passions.... Stated more boldly, people act and sound as though they are strongly motivated by their material self-interest because scientific theories and collective representations derived from those theories convince them that it is natural and normal to do so. As Kagan (1989) observed, "People treat self-interest as a natural law and because they believe they should not violate a natural law, they try to obey it." (1059)

To help students recognize that caring is a fundamental human impulse, and even a need, that they share with all other humans, teachers may find it useful to draw on social psychologist Shelley Taylor's *The Tending Instinct*, which argues from an evolutionary perspective and neurological findings that taking care of others "is intrinsic to our nature, at least as vital as the selfishness and aggression that more commonly shape its portrait" (181); it "is as natural, as biologically based, as searching for food or sleeping, and its origins lie deep in our social nature" (10). "Altruism," Taylor finds, "emerges quite naturally from the neurocircuitries for aggression, caregiving, and dominance and from our capacity for bonding.... It's wired in, impulsive in some cases,... nudged by several different neurochemistries" (147), such as oxytocin and EOPs (158). And "the insistent neurochemistry that influences human bonding," she explains, "allows us to tend to strangers as well" (158).

After sketching out these explanations of how helping others is a fundamental human impulse and a way of maintaining one's identity or sense of self, teachers may ask their students to reflect, in journal entries, papers, or class or small-group discussions, on which jobs or other activities of their own they have found most gratifying and what the source of their gratification was. Such reflection and discussion will enhance students' metacognition not only of their own altruistic impulses and actions but also of their more selfish and aggressive impulses and actions, such as defeating an opponent in a competition (athletic, social, or academic). Teachers can then help students recognize how human competition and cooperation are both means to the same end: maintaining a strong identity, or sense of oneself as a force that matters in the world. And from this they can help their students recognize that the same is true of ethnocentrism and cosmopolitanism, which are simply larger, collective forms of competition and cooperation, respectively. To help students recognize these diverse actions as all efforts to support one's identity, teachers may need to draw on research demonstrating how crime, violence, war, terrorism, racism, sexism, and homophobia, as well as other destructive and self-destructive acts, function to maintain identity by establishing oneself as superior to another individual or group. And they may wish as well to inform students of other social psychological research demonstrating how altruistic acts, whether in the form of the work done by Candide and his friends or in the form of working for global justice, can provide a similar and even greater support for one's sense of self. I have provided summaries of much of this work in my *Social Symptoms of Identity Needs*.

In recognizing that their ethnocentric impulses—social dominance, nationalism, and religion (and the forms of violence that they often entail)—are efforts to attain a goal, identity maintenance, that can be met more productively by cosmopolitan actions, students will be poised to choose the latter means to achieve this goal. In this way students can come to see that their own work of a certain sort is a way to avoid poverty, vice, and boredom and perhaps even achieve happiness. Knowledge of the prerequisites of happiness, that is, can help students to examine and develop metacognition of their own aspirations toward elitism and overcome them, replace them with more cosmopolitan aspirations: the desire to work for the common good. The awareness that one is most fulfilled when one does things to help other people in need puts one in touch with the core human ethical impulse that drives cosmopolitan behavior. When students realize that helping others is the most gratifying thing they can do, that it provides in greater degree and with fewer downsides what they also seek from their various forms of ethnocentrism, they will be more inclined to recognize, own, foster, and act upon this cosmopolitanism-enacting ethical impulse.

In summary, the key here is to help students achieve metacognition of both their ethnocentric and their cosmopolitan impulses. This metacognition includes not just an awareness of the impulses in themselves but, crucially, a recognition of how these impulses are efforts to establish and maintain a secure identity, or sense of self. And ideally it will also include the realization that cosmopolitanism is ultimately more fulfilling, and also ethically and logically more defensible, than ethnocentrism. This last realization will be more difficult for many students, because ethnocentrism is a much quicker and easier means of acquiring identity support and hence is often the recourse of first resort when one's identity is weak or threatened. Eschewing ethnocentrism for cosmopolitanism is also made more difficult by the fact that ethnocentrism is advocated and reinforced by nationalism and religion, as discussed above.

It can thus be quite valuable to help students acknowledge how their nationalism and religion both, in somewhat different ways, embody a powerful affirmation of the cosmopolitan impulse in opposition to the ethnocentric impulse that often holds sway in them—to help them recognize, that is, that the same split between the ethnocentric and the cosmopolitan impulse that they themselves embody personally is also present in their nationalism and their religion. The impulse to solidarity is fundamental to both nationalism and religion in that both emphasize collective identity—the nation and the congregation or communion of saints. The problem is that this collective identity is not universal, all inclusive. Rather, it is exclusionary and oppositional—and hence always potentially violent with respect to people who aren't included in it. In addition to this implicit embrace of a commitment to others, most major religions also contain a strong explicit universalist, cosmopolitan ideal or message, in which not only the highest duty but also the greatest human fulfillment is found in helping others and reducing their suffering.

Metacognition thus culminates in the recognition of what one is truly seeking as a human being and which of various options for living offers the best chance of acquiring what one is seeking.[8] Teachers can support their students' development of this sort of metacognition by helping them reflect on their own impulses and actions of egoism and ethnocentrism on the one hand and altruism and cosmopolitanism on the other, and on the personal and social consequences of each. And through such reflections, students can come to realize that while their ethnocentric impulses may promise a relatively quick and easy form of identity support, they can deliver on this promise only at the cost of a considerable sacrifice of one's intellectual integrity and one's ultimately more fulfilling cosmopolitan impulse, not to mention the sacrifice of the well-being of Others that is inevitably a byproduct of ethnocentrism. And in realizing that ethnocentrism produces a sense of self-worth that is superficial, insubstantial, and largely illusory—consisting of unfounded beliefs in one's superiority with regard to other individuals or groups, in terms of wealth and social status (classism), power (classism and nationalism) and/or a privileged relation to the universe (anthropocentrism/theocentrism)—students will be more inclined toward cosmopolitanism.

Notes

1 For an explanation of how metacognition works and how it can be developed, see Wells.
2 For a fuller explanation of cognitive dissonance, see Cooper.
3 For systematic discussions of these various factors, see Allport 261–282 and Schneider 381–433.
4 Teachers should make sure that their students distinguish this meaning of optimism from simply having a positive outlook on the future, as discussed, for example, in Tali Sharot's book, *The Optimism Bias*.
5 On the nature and power of such resistance, see Alcorn.
6 The text itself, of course, does not make the case for cosmopolitanism at this point. Indeed, the farmer himself advocates a kind of isolationism, eschewing all concern with the economic and political realities beyond his small farm,

and Candide and his friends appear to follow suit. But if this point comes up for discussion, both the ethical and the practical problems with this position are fairly easy to demonstrate. On the practical level, the farmer's livelihood—and indeed, his very life and that of his family—are dependent on what happens in the realms of global commerce and politics. And with regard to ethics, ignoring or turning one's back on people in need anywhere in the world is difficult to justify and contrary to the farmer's own ethic of hospitality that he demonstrates with Candide and his friends.

7 I have developed these two points at length in my *Social Symptoms*.
8 For an extended, systematic discussion of how to promote this form of metacognition, see my *Radical Pedagogy*.

5 Correcting Faulty General Person-Schemas with *Things Fall Apart*, "The Old Chief Mshlanga," and *Candide*

Abstract: *In addition to faulty prototypes of specific groups, literary study can also correct faulty general person-schemas that blind us to the Other's need, blamelessness, and common humanity by obscuring four key truths about human existence: (1) that human behavior and life outcomes are often determined more by external circumstances than by the person; (2) that a person's character is determined largely by formative experiences and environments outside the person's control; (3) that all humans possess both good and bad traits—no one is all good or totally bad; and (4) that all humans are interconnected with each other by their common humanity, their mutual interdependence, and innate emotional attunement. Pedagogical practices for correcting the faulty schemas are discussed.*

Mark Bracher. *Educating for Cosmopolitanism: Lessons from Cognitive Science and Literature.* New York: Palgrave Macmillan, 2013. DOI: 10.1057/9781137390202.

A thorough development of cosmopolitan cognition must go beyond the establishment of corrective group prototypes and the development of metacognition. It must also include the establishment of more adequate general person-schemas, or assumptions about human nature, as the default information-processing templates that automatically manage people's perceptions, judgments, and actions concerning other people. These faulty assumptions constitute the core of the Western prototype of the Human that enables the construction of the more particular faulty prototypes of Europeans, Africans, and other Others. But the faulty general person-schemas also operate independently of group prototypes and thus produce faulty and unjust perceptions, judgments, and actions regarding other people even in the absence of stereotypes. And it is these faulty general person-schemas, whether operating independently of specific group prototypes or embedded within them, that prevent us from recognizing the three crucial truths about the Other that elicit empathy and motivate us to help the Other:

1. the Other's suffering or need,
2. the Other's blamelessness for the suffering or need, and
3. the Other's sameness or overlap with ourselves.

Correcting these fundamental assumptions can therefore be crucial not only to achieving more adequate particular schemas of self and others but also to achieving more adequate, cosmopolitan person-perception in general.

My *Literature and Social Justice* provides a fuller treatment of these faulty, harmful schemas and explains how three classic American protest novels—*The Jungle*, *Native Son*, and *The Grapes of Wrath*—operate to help readers replace them with more adequate schemas. But as I note in the final chapter of that book, literary texts that do not marshal a frontal assault on these schemas often contain the seeds of corrective schemas that teachers can nurture through particular pedagogical strategies and assignments. In this chapter I'll explain how this can be done using the texts we've already considered.

Intra-individual heterogeneity

One of these faulty general person-schemas embodies and reproduces the false assumption that individuals are *homogeneous*—that is, either good or bad, savage or civilized, and so on. This assumption is evident, for example, in *Things Fall Apart* in the European missionary Mr. Smith, who "saw things as black and white. And black was evil. He saw the world as a battlefield in which the children of light were locked in mortal conflict with the sons of darkness. He spoke in his sermons about sheep and goats and about wheat and tares. He believed in slaying the prophets of Baal" (184). This assumption of intra-individual homogeneity can be deadly. If (and possibly only if) one believes that it is possible for a human being to be either all good or all bad, savage or civilized, rather than some combination of both, one can rather easily and automatically conclude that one is oneself good and that anyone who differs from oneself in any way is purely and simply bad. And if that is the case, then one has not only the right, but possibly also the duty, to "slay" these who are bad—the "prophets of Baal." This mindset determined not only Mr. Smith's view of Africans but also of Mr. bin Laden's view of Westerners—and Mr. Bush's view of bin Laden and al Qaeda, when he declared that "We" Americans are good, freedom-loving people and "they" are evil people who hate our freedoms: "we" are civilized; "they" are savages.

Contrary to this homogeneity assumption, the truth is that all people everywhere are combinations of good and bad, as David Livingstone concluded with regard to Africans in a statement quoted by Achebe: "I have found it difficult to come to a conclusion on their [African] character. They sometimes perform actions remarkably good, and sometimes as strangely the opposite.... After long observation, I came to the conclusion that they are just a strange mixture of good and evil as men are everywhere else" (Livingstone, qtd. in Achebe, "Africa's" 217). To facilitate recognition of this truth and prevent the division of the world into a good "us" and an evil "them," it is crucial to replace the person-schema of homogeneity with that of *heterogeneity*, which recognizes that every person is complex, composed of multiple, often conflicting, and sometimes even mutually contradictory qualities, including good and evil, savagery and civility. Prototypes of ethnic groups, as well as of the Human itself, that reflect this fact will do much to prevent, or at least moderate, polarizations between own group and outgroups.

Teachers can promote the development of the *heterogeneity* schema to replace the homogeneity schema by advising students to *expect* every character—and person—they encounter to embody both good and bad qualities, to *attend to* both types of qualities in every character or person they encounter, to *search for* them when they are not manifest, to *infer* them from indirect evidence when they are not explicit, to *suppose* them in the absence of all evidence, and to *encode* them in memory as exemplars of heterogeneity. Equipped with the expectation of heterogeneity, students will readily find it in *Things Fall Apart*, in Okonkwo as well as in characters such as Nwoye and Ezinma. A little searching will turn up both positive and negative qualities in other characters, such as Ekwefi (a devoted mother but at times a less than faithful spouse). Students will also be able, with some effort, to infer qualities that are not directly evident—noting, for example, that though the Europeans in the novel are obtuse and brutal in their treatment of the Ibo, the years they have spent in a foreign and (to them) dangerous land would seem to indicate the presence of some virtues such as courage and perseverance and possibly even altruism and self-sacrifice (albeit of a perniciously benighted sort).

Students can uncover a similar heterogeneity in "The Old Chief Mshlanga." It is present, for example, in the narrator, who behaves with callous disregard and even cruelty toward the Africans but also, somewhat later, comes to feel respect and sympathy for them. Through her eyes, readers are also able to see the heterogeneity of Africans and Europeans generally. Africans, despite being more "primitive" than Europeans in certain aspects of "civilization," such as science and technology, are shown to be more advanced than Europeans in other respects, such as their ethos of peaceful and sustainable coexistence with the land and even with the European invaders. And conversely, the Europeans are shown to be ethically savage in their use of the land and their authoritarian and inhumane treatment of Chief Mshlanga and his people. Chief Mshlanga evinces considerably greater dignity and humanity than the narrator's father, for example.

Candide can also be used to develop the general person-schema of heterogeneity. Though here as in "Mshlanga" the heterogeneity tends to be intra-group rather than intra-individual per se, the result is a revision of the schema of the Human from homogeneous to heterogeneous. The prototype of Westerners as homogeneously civilized and rational is countered on virtually every page of *Candide* by exemplars of Europeans who are irrational and savage, driven by pride, vanity, lust, and greed to commit all sorts of acts of ingratitude, treachery, aggression, and violence against their fellows. The multiple corrupt clerics constitute, by virtue of their irony of character, a particularly salient group of exemplars of heterogeneity. Though there are fewer exemplars of counter-stereotypic non-European Others, Cacambo is a very prominent figure and embodies the civilized qualities of honesty, trustworthiness, loyalty, intelligence, and rationality. The same is true of the Eldoradoans.

Universal solidarity

A second faulty person-schema, that of atomism, embodies the false assumption that each individual is fundamentally separate from other individuals, self-enclosed like an atom, a monad, a billiard ball. In this view, individuals are purely self-interested and self-serving, often at the expense of other individuals. Atomism embodies the Hobbesian view that life is a war of each against all, for which relations with others are purely instrumental, and altruistic acts are merely strategies for self-advancement. But although humans are certainly self-interested and often behave with little or no apparent regard for anyone but themselves, they are also intrinsically and inextricably interwoven with other individuals. Atomism overlooks the fact that an individual's self extends beyond the individual to include, in varying degrees, all other human beings. This solidarity takes three basic forms (see Davis et al. 714). First, there is ontological solidarity, the fact that human being is fundamentally the same from one individual to another, since we all share the same basic anatomy and physiology, including brain structure, and hence also the same basic physical and psychological needs, vulnerabilities, and capabilities. The second form of solidarity is neuro-cognitive, the fact that our brains contain "mirror neurons," which make us resonate physiologically and emotionally with the feelings and actions of other people, a process that we experience as empathy (see Iacoboni). And third is practical solidarity, the fact that we are all mutually interdependent in numerous ways for our survival and well-being. Thus all humans are interwoven with each other, in three basic ways: (1) there is a universal human nature—our "species-being," as Marx called it, which includes our common anatomical and brain structures—that underlies all our differences from each other,[1] and this universal human nature includes (2) the universal ability (and inclination) to empathize and identify with all other humans and (3) to help them when they are in distress (see Chapter 4). Recognizing these three types of solidarity is central to cosmopolitanism, for awareness of even one of these types is sufficient to produce an acknowledgment of self-other overlap, which, as we have seen, is a prerequisite for compassion. In other words, we can ignore the Other's overlap with ourselves only if we refuse to recognize *any* mode of universal human solidarity.

Teachers can promote the development of a solidarity person-schema to replace the schema of atomism by helping students recognize and encode various exemplars of each type of solidarity. In teaching *Things Fall Apart*, they can promote recognition of ontological solidarity by emphasizing the Other's common humanity in the ways described in Chapter 3 and pointing out that this humanity common to Europeans and Africans extends to all other humans as well. When asked to find exemplars of neuro-cognitive solidarity, students can easily find them in the form of characters' love, emotional attachment, and empathy for each other, such as Okonkwo's and Ekwefi's love for each other and for Ezinma, Okonkwo's need for validation from his village (indicated by his quest for titles), Okonkwo's throwing a feast for the people of Mbanta before he returns to Umuofia at the end of his exile, and Okonkwo's concern for the clan and his struggle to prevent it from falling apart. Exemplars of practical solidarity will also be easy for students to find. These include share-cropping (through which Okonkwo got his start), Unoka's borrowing money, Mbanta's receiving the exiled Okonkwo, Obierika's looking after Okonkwo's assets during his exile, and the division of labor among and within families in the village.

In "The Old Chief Mshlanga," students will be able to recognize the chief's dignity and civility during his initial encounter with the narrator, as well as her recognition of them, as evidence of ontological solidarity, or their common humanity. And with some help, they will also be able to register her recognition of his dignity as an instance of psychological solidarity or attunement. Asked to identify examples of practical solidarity, students should be able to come up with the mutual, though highly asymmetrical, reliance of the settlers and the natives (the settlers relying on the natives for labor and the natives depending on the settlers for jobs) and generalize this relationship to an understanding of how even imperial and colonizing powers are dependent on their subalterns in all sorts of ways.

When prompted to search for similar practical solidarity in *Candide*, students will also be able to identify examples of the asymmetrical impact of colonizer and colonized on each other in the form of the baron's sumptuous meal versus the subsistence fare of the indigenous peasants, and the missing hand and leg of the black slave versus the sugar that

Europeans consume. A more symmetrical example of practical solidarity is present at the novel's end in the division of labor among Candide and his friends. Emotional solidarity can be found in the various acts of empathy and kindness performed by Candide as well as, occasionally, by other characters such as James the Anabaptist. Ontological solidarity is less overt but may be inferred from the novel's recognition of the general bleakness of the human condition, as indicated in the Old Woman's disquisition on the brutalities of life and by Candide's recognition at the end that even kings and emperors are subject to the whims of fortune.

Situatedness and malleability

The final two false assumptions about persons in general are autonomism and essentialism. Autonomism (or dispositionism, as psychologists call it) is the assumption that people's behaviors and their life outcomes are determined by their character and that circumstances make little or no difference. Essentialism, as I am using the term, refers to the view that a person's character is fixed at birth rather than produced by one's upbringing, or formative environment. Substantial psychological and social research has refuted both autonomism and essentialism. Studies have shown, for example, that the situation people are in often trumps their character in determining their behavior (Ross and Nisbett; Zimbardo) and that people's formative environments play a greater role than their genetic endowment in determining the kind of person they become (Garbarino).

Recognizing these two truths—situatedness and malleability, respectively—about people is often critical for recognizing their common humanity and overlap with oneself, because it is these two principles that make it possible to understand how the Other can be fundamentally the same as oneself despite presenting very different behaviors, life outcomes, and/or character. The principle of situatedness enables us to see that when people's behavior or life outcome is different from ours, it may be because they are, or have been, subjected to circumstances that are very different from ours. That is, it may be that if we had their circumstances, our behavior and/or life outcome would be pretty much like theirs. Of course, often it would not be. Often the reason other people's behavior differs from ours is because their character differs from ours. But in that case it is crucial to understand the reason their character is different from ours—particularly in those instances in which we judge it to be inferior to ours, as when people engage in harmful behaviors that we would not engage in, even in similar circumstances. It is crucial, that is, to recognize that the Other cannot really be blamed for his or her character flaws, because character is not something one can choose; rather, it is something that is formed by the circumstances of one's birth and upbringing.[2]

Thus the judgment that the Other is "fundamentally like me" includes the recognition that where the Other's behavior differs from mine, the reason is not that the Other is fundamentally different from me (e.g., non-human or infrahuman) but rather that the Other's current situation or past (i.e., formative) environment differs or has differed significantly from mine. More specifically, the differences between myself and the Other result from the same basic human nature being operated on by different external forces, which results in different behaviors, modes of consciousness, beliefs, values, and ultimately physical and psychological attributes. And the most substantial differences between two people are recognized to be the result not of a different human nature but of different circumstances (geography, modes of production, etc.), which require different behaviors, modes of consciousness, beliefs, and values and which thus also constitute a different formative environment that produces different characteristics, and hence character.

As with the other person-schemas, teachers can promote the development of the situatedness schema by helping their students recognize exemplars of situatedness and commit them to memory. They can start by instructing their students to expect, search for, focus on, infer, suppose, and commit to memory the impact of circumstances on all actions and life outcomes. In *Things Fall Apart*, Okonkwo is the most prominent exemplar of situatedness. The novel itself prompts readers to think about this issue concerning Okonkwo in particular by raising the question of how much of a man's behavior and success are to be attributed to his *chi*, which Achebe has translated as one's personal god or spirit (Achebe, "Interview" 126). Okonkwo's successes as a wrestler, as a farmer, as a warrior, and as an *egwugwu* are clearly due to his hard work, fierce determination, and perseverance. At the same time, however, a different set of circumstances at any point along any of his paths to these successes could have rendered all his efforts futile, as the weather did his first attempt at farming. Stronger opponents in wrestling or war, or a misstep at any point in these struggles, could have resulted in a completely different outcome in these areas as well. Even more notably, his failures and setbacks are the product of circumstances beyond his control. These include the oracle's decree that Ikemefuna should be put to death, the explosion of Okonkwo's gun, the arrival of the Europeans, the unmasking and hence (it is believed) killing of the *egwugwu*, and the effrontery of the messenger that Okonkwo beheads. Circumstances play an equally central role in Okonkwo's behaviors, including his violence. His violent acts, while often injudicious and unjustifiable, are never simply gratuitous; they are always triggered by a very real threat to Okonkwo or to things he cares about.

Instances of situatedness in "Mshlanga" are crucial for the narrator's growing recognition of the humanity of the chief and his people, and when tasked to do so, students should be able to identify most of them. In the absence of her chance encounter with Mshlanga on the path, or the presence in her family's library of books attesting to his greatness, or her finding the chief's village with him present in it, or the incident with the goats, or the presence of the chief's son as the family's cook, the narrator might not have gained her new understanding of the chief and of herself and, more broadly, of Africans and Europeans. Other examples of the impact of circumstances on behavior or life outcomes include the alienation and panic experienced by the girl—and by Europeans in general, we are told—when she is alone on the veld on her way to the chief's village, and, much more consequentially, the effect of the Europeans' invasion and actions on the chief and his people and other Africans as well.

Candide is replete with instances of situatedness. Indeed, luck and chance determine the characters' actions and fate at every turn. Candide himself experiences multiple reversals of fate during the first few chapters alone as a result of chance encounters with Cunegonde (they kiss), her father (he sees them kissing and evicts Candide), the impressment officers (they feed him and then conscript him), his commanding officer (who subjects him to running the gauntlet), the king (who gives him a reprieve), James the Anabaptist (who feeds him and gives him a job), Pangloss (who recommences his indoctrination of Candide and prevents him from saving the drowning James), and Cunegonde and the Old Woman, who rescue him from the Inquisition. Other prominent victims of circumstance include Cunegonde and the rest of her family, who are variously raped, butchered, and killed during the war; the Old Woman, who is subjected to a much longer series of brutalizations stretching across her entire adult life; and Martin, who wins Candide's competition for the most unfortunate person.

Of particular significance in *Candide* is the determinative force exerted on people's behavior by authority and peer pressure. Candide's deferral to Pangloss's claim that James was meant to drown in the Lisbon harbor is a striking example of the power of authority to determine behavior. Less obvious but more insidious is the authority of custom and tradition and its power to make individuals do equally absurd and terrible things. The most significant example of this is the mindless acceptance of war and the various brutalities it involves simply because that's the way things have always been done. These brutalities are acquiesced in not only by the perpetrators but also by the victims—most notably Cunegonde and the Old Woman, whose initial resistance to being raped and brutalized in other ways dissolves when they realize that these brutalities are customary.

Promoting students' development of the malleability person-schema can be accomplished in the same fundamental way: by instructing them to expect, focus on, search for, infer, suppose, and commit to memory the various environmental factors that form, and in some cases re-form, the character of various individuals, real and fictional. That Okonkwo has been significantly formed—and also malformed and deformed—by his upbringing is expressly stated and powerfully demonstrated by *Things Fall Apart*. As we noted in Chapter 3, his violent character is largely if not totally the product of his shame regarding his father's cowardice, ineffectuality, and ignominy. If these stigmas of his father had been absent, Okonkwo would have no doubt been a different man. Similarly, if Okonkwo had been different, or had at least treated his son Nwoye less harshly, Nwoye's character might also have been significantly different, resulting, perhaps, in his rejecting Christianity rather than embracing it.

Apart from helping students recognize the impact of formative environments on individual characters, teachers can also engage them in reflecting on how differences in group characteristics derive not from different fundamental natures or genetic endowments but rather from differences in formative environment—in this case, geographical differences, which demand the development of different capabilities, interests, desires, beliefs, values, laws, rituals, rules, and roles in order for the group to survive. Here teachers might draw on historical analyses such as Jared Diamond's *Guns, Germs, and Steel: The Fates of Human Societies* to help students understand that the reason Europe invaded, conquered, enslaved, and colonized Africa and other continents—rather than vice versa—is not because they were a superior form of humanity, as Westerners have liked to think, but rather because Europe possessed unique geographical characteristics that facilitated the development of various technologies, agricultural practices, diseases, and immunities that gave them significant advantages over peoples living in other places on the planet.

Students can be asked to find exemplars of such consequences of the formative environment in "The Old Chief Mshlanga." They should be able to notice immediately how the young girl's attitudes and perceptions regarding not only the African natives but also the very landscape have been formed by her Eurocentric environment and upbringing, as discussed in the previous chapter. A second, equally significant exemplar of malleability is the transformation of her perception and attitudes as a result of her present environment and experiences. And this transformation includes the awareness of a third exemplar of malleability: the fact that the Africans and their culture and civilization have been formed at a deep level by their interaction with the geographical features of Africa, an interaction that the narrator imagines as "a slow intimate dance of landscape and men, a very old dance, whose steps I could not learn" (1479).

Candide provides exemplars of three basic types of transformation: epiphanic, transformation resulting from a flash of insight or recognition; traumatic, transformation (or deformation) resulting from either an acute or chronic assault on the integrity of the self; and incremental, a (re-)formation resulting from the repeated enactment, over time, of certain actions or modes of being in response to a certain ongoing set of circumstances, such as a job, a relationship, or a financial or political position. Transformative epiphanies in *Candide* include various experiences that dramatically refute Pangloss's optimism, most notably the encounter with the dervish and the subsequent conversation with the old farmer, two events that convince Candide to renounce Panglossian philosophizing and cultivate his garden instead. Incremental and also traumatic transformation can be seen in the backgrounds of the Old Woman and Martin, whose demoralizing and horrifying life experiences have turned them into pessimists, and also in Candide's (though agonizingly slow) distancing from Pangloss's views.

More interesting and significant than these intra-textual instances of malleability, however, are the possible instances of transformation resulting in students themselves, as a result of reading and discussing this text. Some students may have various types and degrees of epiphany concerning their own ethnos or their ethnocentrism—that is, their religion, nationality, or race, and their attendant chauvinism concerning these identities. Other students may experience a kind of trauma when confronted with the text's iconoclasm and cultural relativism. And some students may experience a gradual alteration of their beliefs or attitudes as a result of the cumulative effects of the text's episodes. Teachers can establish these various types and instances as exemplars of malleability by asking for volunteers to describe any of these three types of reaction that they may have had to the text and then helping the class recognize these experiences as exemplars of malleability and encode them as such.

Conclusion

To maximize the correction of faulty person-schemas, it is useful to teach texts such as these, which provide less overt challenges to the faulty schemas than many protest novels do. Encountering less obvious instances of the corrective information and/or exemplars for revising or replacing faulty schemas affords the opportunity to develop students' ability to activate and utilize the corrective schemas with less help from external sources, such as a literary text. A further step along this path involves texts that accept or endorse the faulty, harmful schemas. Reading such texts between the lines or against the grain provides training in using the corrective schemas when there is little or no external support, and perhaps even opposition—whether in a literary text or in public discourse—for the more comprehensive and accurate perception and judgment of others. Virtually any literary text—that is, any text with characters or personae—can be deconstructed along these lines, reading its margins and silences concerning the situatedness, formative environments, heterogeneity, and solidarity of its characters/personae.

Notes

1. On this point, which many humanists in recent decades have rejected, see Pinker; Eagleton; and Todorov.
2. At whatever point in our development we might legitimately be said to "choose" to be a certain kind of person, including good or bad, the self that makes this choice has already been determined for us: it is the self that was constructed by forces beyond our control or even our understanding.

6
Developing Cosmopolitan Action Scripts with Camus's "The Guest" and Coetzee's *Disgrace*

Abstract: *Thoroughgoing cosmopolitanism includes taking action, and in order to act on their compassion for the Other, individuals must possess plans or scripts for meeting the Other's needs. Literary study can promote the development of and investment in such scripts. This chapter explains how teachers can employ "The Guest" to help students develop a script of global hospitality that involves providing for needy Others everywhere even at some cost to oneself, and how* Disgrace *can be taught in a manner that develops the most difficult and thoroughgoing of cosmopolitan action scripts, that of sacrificing one's own wealth, power, security—and perhaps even one's very being, identity, self-integrity—for the benefit of needy Others whose beliefs, values, and behaviors one may find antithetical to one's own.*

Mark Bracher. *Educating for Cosmopolitanism: Lessons from Cognitive Science and Literature.* New York: Palgrave Macmillan, 2013. DOI: 10.1057/9781137390202.

Compassion for distant Others may be a crucial element of cosmopolitanism, but it is not by itself sufficient to produce the advancements in global justice that constitute the central purpose of cosmopolitanism. True cosmopolitanism involves not just having feelings of sympathy or altruistic inclinations regarding the Other; it also involves taking effective action to advance global justice. And for people to take such action, they must be cognizant of a viable path leading from here to there: studies have shown that awareness of a feasible means of helping people one desires to help is a prerequisite for altruistic action (see Ross and Nisbett). True cosmopolitans must thus possess an action script, a plan for a course of action that will advance global justice.

People develop action scripts by rehearsing them in various ways, including observing—or reading about—other people taking a particular action, and also by engaging in the action themselves, or imagining doing so.[1] Literary study can help to develop action scripts by engaging students in rehearsing them in several of these ways, including reading about them, discussing them, and writing about them. And literary study can develop cosmopolitan action scripts by nurturing the four corrective general person-schemas and then linking the understanding of, and compassion for, the Other that these schemas produce to action scripts of helping distant strangers and promoting global justice. In what follows, I will explain how this process can be implemented through teaching Camus's "The Guest" and Coetzee's *Disgrace*.

Cosmopolitanism as hospitality: "The Guest"

Camus's short story "The Guest" offers teachers an opportunity to enhance their students' capabilities of discerning the four key features of human existence in distant Others and linking the compassion that such discernment generates to the basic cosmopolitan action script of hospitality: providing food, drink, shelter, and other necessities for people in need throughout the world. The story also engages the readers in an imaginative rehearsal of this script in a concrete and rudimentary form. Its basic plot consists of the French schoolmaster Daru's feeding, providing for, and setting free the Arab prisoner that the authorities have tasked him with delivering to another jail. Along the way, the text also exemplifies the four key features of human existence the recognition of which, as we have seen, is a prerequisite for accurate and just actions regarding the Other: solidarity, heterogeneity, situatedness, and malleability. By assigning students the tasks of (a) locating and articulating these exemplifications, (b) explaining how these principles are true of the Arab prisoner, and (c) reflecting on how these features of the prisoner entail Daru's hospitality toward him, teachers can help their students develop not only more robust corrective person-schemas but also, embedded in these schemas, a compassionate action script of care and hospitality for the Other.

Seeking exemplifications of the corrective principles

The first step of this assignment—locating and articulating textual evidence of the four corrective principles—will engage students in practicing corrective information-processing routines. That is, they will engage in expecting, searching for, perceiving, attending to, inferring, supposing, encoding in memory, and recalling from memory instances of situatedness, malleability, solidarity, and heterogeneity. Students can be engaged in these cognitive practices either by having them search the text for evidence supporting one of the principles (they can be divided into groups, with each group focusing on a different principle) or by identifying particular episodes, actions, or passages in the text and asking students which of the four principles it exemplifies.

One can introduce the four corrective principles by asking students to reflect on the significance of the story's title. Some students may observe—and if they do not, the teacher can point out—that the original, French title, "L'hôte," can mean not only "guest" but also "host." Noting that Camus was a prominent existentialist writer concerned with exploring the most fundamental parameters of human existence, the teacher can ask the class what basic features of human existence the author may be gesturing toward with this title. In what ways, that is, might all humans be seen as both hosts and guests? To help answer this question, teachers can pose two other questions: what examples of guests and hosts does the text offer, and what are the essential elements of guest and host embodied in these examples? By directing the ensuing discussion, teachers can bring the class to recognize how human existence involves, at its most basic level, being both a guest and a host in relation to others, and how this guest/host position entails the four principles of situatedness, malleability, solidarity, and heterogeneity.

Human situatedness

The story's most prominent exemplars of host and guest are Daru and the Arab prisoner. And their interaction indicates the essentials of the two positions: a host is someone who provides food, drink, and shelter for another person who is dependent on him for these necessities. Does it make sense, the teacher may ask, to say that these two positions are fundamental to all humans? It will not be hard for students to acknowledge that every individual is fundamentally a guest at the beginning of life, being totally dependent on others for food and shelter. And with a little help, it will not be difficult for the class to recognize that virtually all humans remain to some degree dependent on others for food and shelter throughout their life, insofar as they don't individually produce and prepare all their food or construct their shelter from scratch with tools they personally invented and manufactured from scratch. Asked to find examples of this point in the text, students can point to the fact that both Daru and his students are dependent on grain grown, harvested, and imported to their region by others.

Teachers can then ask their students to explore the implications of this fact: what does the dependence on others for one's food, in this story and generally, say about the human condition? Through discussion of this question, students can be helped to recognize the general principle of situatedness: the fact that all humans are always, in one way or another, subject in their actions and life outcomes to circumstances beyond their control. These circumstances include the actions of other humans as well as non-human factors such as geography (including climate) and weather. Some students may recognize this principle in the fact that Daru's region is dependent on supplies from Tadjid and wheat imports from France because the rocky landscape and the drought have made it impossible for the inhabitants to grow enough food to feed themselves (1512–1513). It may also be observed that these circumstances, which have resulted in the deaths of thousands of sheep and even a number of people in the region, are in all likelihood a key cause of the Arab prisoner's killing his cousin in an argument over grain (1515). In the absence of the drought and famine, it is likely that the prisoner would not have killed his cousin and that Daru would then not have been saddled with the prisoner.

The fact that other people and their actions often constitute key elements of situations is also evident in the text. Students can observe that the presence and behavior of the prisoner's cousin were essential determinants of the prisoner's action and his consequent life outcome. Similarly, the actions of the police who tracked the prisoner down and extracted him from the protection of his relatives, and the decision of the authorities to hand him over to Daru for transfer to Tinguit, are essential factors in the situation that Daru now finds himself in through no action, choice, or fault of his own—a situation that may ultimately result in his murder at the hands of the prisoner's relatives (see 1520). In addition, all of this action takes place within the larger political context of French colonialism and the incipient uprising of the indigenous Algerians.

Human malleability

Students should also be able to locate several examples of human malleability, indications by the text of the formative impact that a host environment has on human character. The text hints, for example, that the cruel environment, inhospitable to human habitation, may make its human inhabitants somewhat cruel as well: "the region was...cruel to live in, even without men—who didn't help matters either" (1513). More generally, the text suggests that the desolate geography of the region has formed both Daru and the prisoner, educing in them a subjective correlative to the material features of the landscape and climate. Daru was born in the region, we are told, and "everywhere else, he felt exiled" (1513). And after living on the barren plateau for some years, he has also become acclimated to its harshness. When he first moved to this host location,

> the solitude and the silence had been hard for him on these wastelands peopled only by stones. Occasionally, furrows suggested cultivation, but they had been dug to uncover a certain kind of stone good for building. The only plowing here was to harvest rocks. Elsewhere a thin layer of soil accumulated in the hollows would be scraped out to enrich paltry village gardens. This is the way it was: bare rock covered three quarters of the region. Towns sprang up, flourished, then disappeared; men came by, loved one another or fought bitterly, then died. No one in this desert, neither he nor his guest, mattered. And yet, outside this desert neither of them, Daru knew, could have really lived. (1516)

The fact that Daru is a schoolmaster and that the schoolhouse he occupies serves as a kind of prison for the Arab points, in addition, to the formative and even subjugating effects of education specifically and enculturation generally. More specifically, the subjugating effects of colonialism are indicated by the fact, mentioned in both the second and the final paragraph of the story, that the classroom's blackboard contains a drawing of the four rivers of France, suggesting that the Algerian students are being indoctrinated with French culture at the expense of their own. And it may be that the resulting hegemony of things French and European in the mind of the prisoner plays a role in his choosing, at the end of the story, the path to prison rather than to freedom.

Intra-individual heterogeneity

Intra-individual heterogeneity is evidenced by the text in several ways. The general principle is exemplified in the dual meaning of the title, L'hôte, which indicates that every individual is both host and guest. That is, every individual, as we have already discussed, is dependent on and subject to other individuals as well as the physical world. Conversely, every individual is also responsible for the welfare of others. This responsibility can be seen, most minimally and fundamentally, in the fact that every individual takes up space and consumes resources that others also need and may thereby be deprived of—as the fatal quarrel between the prisoner and his cousin demonstrates all too clearly. In addition, humans are also responsible for each other by virtue of their very dependence on others, a dependence that exerts an emotional tug on the other. And just as humans are dependent on and subject to physical nature, so too are they responsible for it, in that it requires human action (e.g., in the form of agriculture) to bear maximum fruit, and needs human restraint (in the form of environmentalism) in order to survive.

Such reflections may be too abstract and abstruse for some students, but they will have little difficulty in recognizing the more specific intra-individual heterogeneity of both Daru and the prisoner. Daru himself occupies the opposing positions of guest (as a Frenchman in Algeria) and host (as a schoolteacher, he is host to his students). Other dimensions of Daru's heterogeneity include his opposing feelings of compassion and wrath toward the Arab and his considerate and inconsiderate behaviors toward the gendarme Balducci. And his freeing of the prisoner can be seen as both a generous act (giving another human being freedom) and a selfish act (freeing himself of a burden).

It should also be fairly easy for students to identify heterogeneity in the prisoner. Most notable is the combination of violence and docility: he has killed his cousin by slitting his throat with a billhook, but he is completely docile and even passive in Daru's presence, to the point of returning to the schoolhouse when, after stealthily exiting it in the middle of the night to relieve himself, he could easily have escaped, as well as heading to jail in Tinguit rather than taking refuge with the nomads.

Solidarity

"The Guest" also demonstrates human solidarity in a number of significant ways. The title signals all three types of solidarity. The universal host/guest relationship is one of practical solidarity: all humans are mutually interdependent, both giving and getting resources from others that are essential for living. The fact that this interdependence characterizes all humans marks an important dimension of ontological solidarity, or sameness. And insofar as the host is motivated by sympathy and compassion, hosting also invokes emotional solidarity.

The text also indicates these dimensions of solidarity more concretely. The mutual interdependence that constitutes practical solidarity is manifest in Daru's reliance on his pupils for his job and their dependence on him for their education as well as for the grain for their families, for which both they and Daru are also reliant on a host of other hosts, ranging from the farmers who grow and harvest it to the shippers who transport it. Practical solidarity is also present in the relationships between and among Daru, the prisoner, and Balducci: the actions of each have important consequences for the other.

Students should be able to identify a number of ways in which Daru has an ontological solidarity with the prisoner. For one, the two share certain traits, such as obstinacy (1513, 1514) and anger/aggression (1515). In addition, they are both subject to the dictates of the authorities, and they also share the basic human physical needs, including the need for food, drink, and sleep. The fact that they eat, drink, and sleep together, in the same room, emphasizes this commonality. And the text suggests that the insistence of this common humanity, or ontological solidarity, produces a kind of psychological solidarity as well, in the form of an emotional bond that imposes itself (much as, in the ethics of Emanuel Lévinas, responsibility for the other is said to do):

> In this room where he had been sleeping alone for a year, this presence [of the prisoner] bothered him. But it bothered him also by imposing on him a sort of brotherhood he knew well but refused to accept in the present

circumstances. Men who share the same rooms, soldiers or prisoners, develop a strange alliance as if, having cast off their armor with their clothing, they fraternized every evening, over and above their differences, in the ancient community of dream and fatigue. (1518)

Corrective exemplars and prototypes of the human

In expecting, seeking out, perceiving, attending to, inferring, and articulating these textual indicators of human solidarity, heterogeneity, malleability, and situatedness, students will develop information-processing scripts—capabilities and habits of cognition—that with further practice can become the default routines for perceiving and judging other people, thus leading to the three key, compassion-producing judgments that are central to cosmopolitan cognition: recognizing the Other's need, the Other's lack of blame for the need, and the Other's overlap with oneself. In addition, these cognitive activities also contribute, as we discussed in detail with *Things Fall Apart*, to the formation of more adequate general person-prototypes, by adding corrective exemplars—Daru and the prisoner, in the present case—to students' long-term memory. Daru and the prisoner, that is, through the foregoing analyses, emerge as exemplars of situatedness, malleability, heterogeneity, and solidarity. These exemplars, in turn, can themselves serve as templates for perceiving and judging other people and also contribute, through accretion with other exemplars, to the formation of the more adequate prototypes of the human, those of situatedness, malleability, heterogeneity, and solidarity.

Deriving action scripts from the adequate perception of the Other

Helping students develop the general person-schemas of situatedness, malleability, heterogeneity, and solidarity, then, enables them to recognize the Other's need, blamelessness, and overlap with themselves, and these judgments result in a feeling of compassion for the Other. This emotion of compassion, in turn, will incline them to address the other's need, the action tendency that is inherent in compassion (see Chapter 2). But for this inclination to become an effective action, students must have ready access to a script for an action that will deliver aid to the Other. In the absence of a realistic script that is readily accessible to consciousness, the action tendency can easily die without any action taking place. Thus one of the most important things that educators can do to promote cosmopolitanism is to help students develop action scripts for providing relief to distant strangers and advancing justice without boundaries. And literary texts such as "The Guest" and *Disgrace*, which sketch out such action scripts, can serve as the basis for such development.

In the case of "The Guest," the basic action is that of Daru's hosting, or hospitality. Daru's acts of hospitality include freeing the prisoner from his bonds (asking Balducci to untie him), giving him tea to quench his thirst, feeding him dinner to assuage his hunger, providing him shelter in the schoolhouse, setting up a bed with blankets for him to sleep on, feeding him breakfast, preparing a package of food for him to eat on his journey, providing him with 1,000 francs with which to meet future contingencies, and educating him regarding the courses of action available to him and their corresponding consequences—that is, the respective paths to freedom and bondage.

Teachers can help students articulate these acts of the hospitality script that constitutes the basic action of cosmopolitanism: addressing the Other's needs, beginning with the most basic needs for food, water, and shelter, but also including the most human, psychological or spiritual, needs, including freedom and respect, here enacted in Daru's providing the prisoner with the freedom to choose his own path. Teachers may wish to point out that this cosmopolitan script is identical in its essentials with some prominent ethical directives, including Jesus' admonition to feed the hungry, give drink to the thirsty, and provide shelter for the stranger and succor for the prisoner (see Matthew 25: 31–45). It is also important for students to recognize that Daru's hospitality is enacted at some cost to himself: in releasing the prisoner, he is transgressing the law, or at least disobeying the orders of the authorities, and he has also inadvertently made himself the object of a severe threat from the prisoner's kin.

In order for students to commit this basic script to memory as a viable and desirable template for acting on their compassion, they will need to rehearse and elaborate it. And they will need to examine, and explore their feelings about, the likely costs and benefits to themselves and others of enacting the hospitality script in various ways and contexts. This can involve the relative costs and benefits produced by various government policies and agencies, as well as those of NGOs that one might support financially and in other ways. Such a discussion may be initiated by or supplemented with readings from cosmopolitan ethicists such as Peter Singer (*The Life You Can Save: How to Do Your Part to End World Poverty*) or cosmopolitan economists such as Jeffrey Sachs (*The End of Poverty: Economic Possibilities for Our Time*).

But in addition to the financial costs of higher taxes or charitable donations, the cosmopolitan action of hospitality can also exact other costs. It may, as it does for Daru, involve opposing the policies or directives of one's own government officials, and it may also elicit opposition from elements of the Other, such as foreign governments or contingents. Students may be asked to consider instances where U.S. aid is impeded or prevented by armed forces in the location of delivery: what costs, including U.S. military action, would they be willing to bear in order to save the lives of people in distant lands? Would they be willing to sacrifice billions of tax dollars, dozens, hundreds, or possibly thousands of American lives, or even their own lives in order to provide life-saving aid (food, potable water, medical supplies, sanctuary) for distant strangers, Others? In each case, it is important to help students recognize and articulate fully the situatedness, malleability, heterogeneity, and solidarity of the Other under consideration. The crucial point here is for students to achieve full awareness of the Other's need, blamelessness, and overlap with themselves, and then to become aware of their feelings of compassion for the Other and of the various viable actions they might take to meet the Other's needs and consider, as they dwell in their compassion for the Other, what degree of sacrifice they might be willing to make to provide such care for the Other. By imagining taking political or philanthropic action of this sort, students will establish an action script that, the more they imagine it, and thereby rehearse it, the more it will become capable of actually motivating and directing their response to strangers in need throughout the world.[2]

Cosmopolitanism as the relinquishment of power: Coetzee's *Disgrace*

While the action script of hospitality can do much to alleviate the suffering of distant Others, it is never carried as far as it needs to be to adequately address global suffering and injustice. It is enacted too inconsistently and inadequately to meet the needs of the billions of suffering people who inhabit the planet. The problem is not that the planet does not produce enough food, water, and other materials to take care of all its inhabitants but rather that those of us with the wealth and power to meet those needs have not made it a priority to do so (see Sachs).

The reason we have not done so is the recognition that it would prove costly for us. How far should our hospitality go? Should it include not only considerable financial costs but also massive redistribution of our wealth and power? And should such self-dispossession include not only loss of money, property, and personal security, but the sacrifice of one's life, one's identity, one's self-integrity, one's very being, as well? This last question confronts us when the Other's difference from ourselves may be so severe as to constitute immorality, inhumaneness, and even inhumanity—including toward ourselves and our loved ones.[3]

Global justice clearly requires more action from the haves than simply occasional provision of material necessities to the have-nots. While such actions often ameliorate misery and destitution of numerous individuals, they do very little to mitigate the obscene structural inequalities whereby Americans, for example, with 5 percent of the world's population, consume 25 percent of the world's fossil fuels. For Westerners, a thoroughgoing cosmopolitanism will ultimately require both providing greater systematic sustenance and structural assistance to the Other and also ceding power and wealth to the Other. And such self-dispossession may mean handing over wealth and power—and perhaps even sacrificing our culture and our very sense of self, or identity—to people whom we may deem less enlightened and even less good than ourselves.

Such redistribution of wealth and power has always been the path—and the major obstacle—to equality and democracy. And resisting this transfer to those whom one judges to be in some way less worthy than oneself has paved the roads of war and genocide and prevented the advancement of global justice. In order to overcome this resistance and formulate action scripts of hospitality and self-dispossession, there are two cognitive prerequisites. First, one must recognize that even if and when the Other embodies beliefs, values, attitudes, and behaviors that are antithetical to one's own, the Other's most fundamental needs—material, social, and psychological—are the same as one's own. And second, one must realize that the qualities of the Other that one finds most objectionable and antithetical to one's own are the product of the historical contingencies of the Other's formative environment and present circumstances, and that the same is true of one's own presumed preferable qualities. The four corrective general person-schemas are critical here, for, as explained previously, they enable the recognition of these truths concerning self and Other: the solidarity schema attunes us to our

DOI: 10.1057/9781137390202

common humanity and deep overlap with the Other; the heterogeneity schema facilitates this recognition by alerting us to positive qualities of the Other (and negative qualities of our own) that may be obscured by the more overt features; the malleability schema emphasizes the Other's lack of responsibility for negative character traits (and our own lack of credit for our positive traits); and the situationism schema directs our attention to factors in the Other's present circumstances that may be variously enabling, eliciting, or coercing certain behaviors of the Other that we find objectionable.

The four corrective general person-schemas thus constitute a virtual prerequisite for the privileged group's voluntary self-dispossession. If those in power can realize the utter contingency not only of their position of power but also of their (supposed) virtue, as well as the historical contingency of the (perceived) powerlessness, ignorance, immorality, and even evil of the Other, they will be able to see that justice requires them both to provide for the Other and also, ultimately, to sacrifice (at least some of) their wealth, their power, and perhaps even their very being to them. And this action script of self-dispossession will enable them to prevent much of the further suffering and injustice that would occur if they were to struggle to maintain their wealth, power, and being in the face of global demographic realities that militate against the West's continued domination.

Thus while the cosmopolitan hospitality script of providing for needy Others throughout the world is challenging enough, this hospitality, when followed to its logical conclusion, entails an even more daunting action: the redistribution of wealth and power. And for those who possess wealth and power—and this means virtually all Westerners, to one degree or another—this requires various types of self-dispossession. Coetzee's novel *Disgrace* provides, in the cognitive and emotional journey of its protagonist, David Lurie, a generalizable script for this most thorough and difficult enactment of cosmopolitanism. And teachers who understand the process by which Lurie arrives at his self-dispossession can help their students emulate Lurie's process and develop their own self-dispossession action scripts. The basic pedagogical strategy here is first, to help students understand the various steps by which Lurie arrives at the point where he embarks upon his self-dispossession and, second, to engage students in cognitive activities—through reading, writing, research, or discussion—that duplicate and rehearse this basic process.

David Lurie's self-dispossession

Lurie's development of a self-dispossession action script begins when his position of domination is challenged by the Other's resistance to his behaviors, beliefs, and/or values. He attempts to justify his domination and exploitation of others by viewing it as natural and right, but he begins to see things from the Other's point of view, and this perspective-taking produces three cognitive consequences: cognitive dissonance, compassion, and guilt. The cognitive dissonance is produced by his realization that the arguments he uses to justify his own sexual exploitation of women could also be used to justify the brutal rape of his daughter Lucy by the three attackers. David's compassion for the Other results from his becoming aware of (a) the Other's suffering or need, (b) the Other's situatedness and malleability—and hence blamelessness for the suffering or need—and (c) the Other's solidarity and heterogeneity, and hence sameness with himself. And his guilt emerges when his perspective-taking reveals to him that his hegemonic identities and the behaviors of his that they have permitted are largely responsible for the Other's suffering and need and ultimately also, in the case of his attackers, the Other's violence toward him and his kind.

The novel takes Lurie—and the reader—through multiple iterations of each step, and never is the process as clear or straightforward as the account I have just given. Rather, Lurie's trajectory is much like that of an analysand in psychoanalysis: he traverses each step multiple times, and in various orders, and the changes in him occur only gradually, sometimes only temporarily, and often virtually invisibly. Only some time after the fact can we see that a significant change has actually occurred, and even then it is often impossible to pinpoint a particular moment or cause of the change. Rather, the change in Lurie occurs as a result of the repetition of certain key cognitions concerning the Other that, over time, produce new capabilities and habits of perception, judgment, feeling, and behavior. By helping students understand this process, and rehearse with Lurie the various instances and forms of each of its steps, teachers can enable them to embark upon this process themselves. And they can strengthen the process through assignments whereby students themselves engage in each of these steps.

Lurie's development of self-dispossession scripts is most obvious and most significant in relation to two Others: first, women, including his student Melanie Isaacs, his daughter Lucy, his ex-wife Rosalind, the prostitutes he hires, and Bev Shaw; and second, indigenous Africans, including the three attackers and, to a lesser degree, Petrus. A third, non-human Other, dogs, also figure prominently in Lurie's development of self-dispossession action scripts.

Following is a sketch of the process that Lurie enacts in response to these Others. Teachers can engage students in emulating this process by first helping them map out one or more of Lurie's enactments of it and then asking them to select an Other of theirs and duplicate Lurie's recognition of the Other's suffering, blamelessness, and sameness with themselves by apprehending, through perspective-taking (which may include some library research), their Other's situatedness, malleability, heterogeneity, and solidarity, followed by the formulation of an action script of self-dispossession of their own.

Women

The most thorough account of Lurie's self-dispossession provided by the novel is that regarding women. Students can be asked to identify instances of Lurie's domination and exploitation of women, followed by noting the resistances he encounters. The resistance of women to his exploitation begins with Soraya's rejection of him after he breaches the prostitute/client boundary by tracking her down and phoning her at home, but it centers on the actions of his student Melanie and her defenders. Through close reading, most students will recognize that Melanie herself resists involvement with him from the beginning. She is at best hesitant to have sex with him on each of the three occasions in which they do so, and in one instance her aversion to the act is so palpable that Lurie feels the need to tell himself that his action did not quite constitute rape (25). Melanie's resistance to his exploitation finally becomes explicit when she files the complaint against him. At this point members of the larger community join the resistance, which culminates in Lurie's being fired.

Students will also note that while there are signs—his pleading guilty to all charges at the hearing, for example—that Lurie may recognize at this early stage that he has exploited Melanie and that the resistance to him is justified, he resists this recognition, attempting to justify himself by claiming that somehow his exploitative and even predatory actions toward Melanie and other women were natural and therefore sacrosanct. In one form of this rationalization, he characterizes his pursuit of women as the action of the gods Aphrodite (25) and Eros (52, 89): "I became a servant of Eros," he tells the committee at the hearing (52). In a slightly more profane version of this argument, he claims that desire itself is sacrosanct, speaking of "the rights of desire" (89) and quoting Blake's proverb from *The Marriage of Heaven and Hell*, "Sooner murder an infant in its cradle than nurse unacted desires" (69). And on another occasion he justifies his seduction of Melanie with the idea that "he is in the grip of... beauty's rose" (18), citing the old line of seduction, "a woman's beauty does not belong to her alone. ... She has a duty to share it" (16).

At this point, teachers may wish to engage their students in the metacognitive activity of reflecting on the ways they, too, may justify their exploitive actions or privileged positions vis-à-vis their Other. Do they attempt, like Lurie, to naturalize their privilege and exploitation? Students can pursue these metacognitive reflections further, exploring the deepest motives underlying their exploitation and privilege by realizing that what is at stake in Lurie's resistance to changing his behavior is much more than mere physical pleasure. Rather, giving up his pursuit of women will mean losing part of himself. As he tells Lucy, "I am not prepared to be reformed. I want to go on being myself" (77). This is a critical point to realize regarding not just Lurie's behavior toward women but also his—and everyone else's—routine behaviors of all sorts: both the behaviors and the enjoyments we get from them can constitute a substantial portion of our personal identity, or sense of self, and as we discussed in Chapter 4, maintaining this identity, or sense of self, is the fundamental motive for all human behavior, including both ethnocentric and cosmopolitan cognition and action. With this understanding, students can begin to recognize how maintaining their positions of dominance in relation to their Others might also be a means of maintaining their identity, or sense of self.

Asked to explain how Lurie's resistance to changing his behavior—and thus also his identity—is worn down, students can chart the path by which he gradually gains a woman's perspective on her experience of his sexual exploitation of her. His first inkling comes in the wake of an unsatisfying sexual encounter with the new secretary Dawn, when he reflects that a "man exercising himself on the body of a woman" is "ugly, from a certain point of view" (9). This realization is reinforced later when his ex-wife Rosalind asks him, "Do you think a young girl finds any pleasure in going to bed with a man of [your] age? Do you think she finds it good to watch you in the middle of your...? Do you ever think about that?" (44). Subsequently, during the hearing, he tries to imagine how the businesswoman on the committee sees him: "What does she see when she looks at him that keeps her at such a pitch of anger? A shark among the helpless little fishies? Or does she have another vision: of a great thick-boned male bearing down on a girl-child, a huge hand stifling her cries?" (53). His first reaction is that such a vision of him would be absurd. "Then he remembers:... Melanie... barely comes to his shoulder. Unequal: how could he deny that?" (53).

Students will have no trouble seeing how Lurie's conversations with his daughter Lucy cause him to wonder about "what women undergo at the hands of men" (111) and thus realize the degree to which he does not understand women. He realizes soon after he arrives at Lucy's smallholding that he can't understand what Lucy sees in her partner Helen (60). After her rape, Lucy and also Bev repeatedly inform him that he doesn't, and possibly can't, understand what happened to her (135, 140, 157). And when he can't understand why Lucy won't leave her smallholding after the rape, she tells him, "You keep misreading me" (112). "I am not the person you know.... You are not the guide I need" 161). He realizes that he may be incapable of imagining what it is like to be a woman being raped (160). Toward the end of the novel, Lucy spells out for him his egocentrism:

> You behave as if everything I do is part of the story of your life. You are the main character, I am a minor character who doesn't make an appearance until halfway through. Well, contrary to what you think, people are not divided into major and minor. I am not minor. I have a life of my own, just as important to me as yours is to you, and in my life I am the one who makes the decisions. (198)

Through these successes and failures in perspective-taking, Lurie gradually acquires some sense of the suffering that women undergo at the hands of men as well as a sense of how women see him. And this new perspective results in a cognitive dissonance that initiates, first, a change in his self-image and then a change in his behavior. Part of him has known from the beginning that his seduction of Melanie is wrong (see 18, 20, 24), and when her father accosts him and accuses him of being a viper, he thinks, "A viper: how can he deny it?" (38). The key event in producing the change in his self-image, however, is the rape of his daughter Lucy by the three indigenous Africans. Lurie's foregoing insensitivity to the experience of rape (and also to the plight of animals) was indicated by his earlier comment to Lucy regarding animal-welfare advocates: "Everyone is so cheerful and well-intentioned that after a while you itch to go off and do some raping and pillaging" (73). Indeed, the very morning of the rape Lurie defends his seduction of Melanie by claiming that he was just following his instincts and that "no animal will accept the justice of being punished for following its instincts" (90). To which Melanie replies: "So males must be allowed to follow their instincts unchecked?" (90). The brutal rape of Lucy only hours later provides the definitive answer to her question, and it is the seed of Lurie's future realization that such brutality is in a sense only the logical culmination of his self-justifying arguments concerning the naturalness and/or divine origin of his own desire. After all, rape, like Eros, is a god: "god of chaos and mixture" (105), as Lurie puts it, without at the time realizing the full significance of his utterance. Lurie never quite views himself as a rapist, but he is moving in that direction when he realizes that, although not as brutal as the rape of Lucy, some of his hero Byron's "seductions" would undoubtedly qualify as rapes (160).

In addition to his growing realization that the supposed "naturalness" of his desire is no justification for acting on it, Lurie also comes to see that from a certain perspective his seduction of Melanie might be seen as unnatural, and that his trial was "for unnatural acts, for broadcasting old seed, tired seed, seed that does not quicken, *contra natura*. If the old men hog the young women, what will be the future of the species? That, at bottom was the case for the prosecution" (190).

As a result of the cognitive dissonance produced by these realizations, Lurie embarks upon a partial self-dispossession of a key part of his identity, or sense of self: his sexual desire and enjoyment, the loss of which he experiences as tantamount to castration and thus in some ways worse than death (see 90). Though this change is not complete or final, it is suggested in his settling, "after the sweet young flesh of Melanie Isaacs" (150) for the "ugly little woman" (84) Bev Shaw, as well as in his prostrating himself at the feet of Melanie's mother and sister even while continuing to desire that sister's young flesh (173), and in his coming to see that he has reached "the end of roaming" (175). How far Lurie's sexual self-dispossession will go—that is, whether it will lead to the (at least metaphorical) self-castration and "the proper business of the old: preparing to die" (9) that he briefly contemplates at the beginning of the novel after unsatisfying assignations with Dawn and the second Soraya—is not clear. But he has definitely embarked upon some degree of self-dispossession as a result of seeing the suffering that women undergo at the hands of men.

Indigenous Africans

The self-dispossession required of Lurie to do justice to his gendered Other is substantial. But that required to do justice to his ethnic Other, indigenous Africans, may be even greater. Certainly their resistance to his hegemony causes him greater trauma. To help students grasp the difficulty of self-dispossession to those who appear morally inferior and even evil, teachers can have them document and explain the trauma Lurie experiences as a result of the brutal attack by the three indigenous African men. The assault leaves him totally shaken, vulnerable, and in despair (107–108), and he fears that Lucy may have had her identity destroyed by the attack: "What if, after an attack like that, one is never oneself again? What if an attack like that turns one into a different and darker person altogether?" (124). And when he learns that Lucy has been impregnated by the rape and that she intends to keep the baby, he feels his own identity, or sense of self, petering out:

> is this how it is all going to end, is this how his line is going to run out, like water dribbling into the earth? .... Suddenly everything is changed, utterly changed.
> Standing against the wall outside the kitchen, hiding his face in his hands, he heaves and heaves and finally cries. (199)

Most students may need help in articulating the exact nature of the identity loss confronting Lurie here. It is the loss of his posthumous being, the sense that some valued part of himself will continue to exist after his death. This sense of loss is heighted by his recent experience of the decline or eclipse of his very culture, in the burglary and looting of his house, the theft and perhaps destruction of important artifacts of European culture (albums of Beethoven and Janacek, 176), and the replacement of his revered poets by applied language studies ("so much for the dead masters," 179). It appears that redistributing power and wealth to the indigenous Africans is going to entail the sacrifice of crucial parts of his identity, or sense of self, in the form of what some psychologists refer to as selfobjects: those things that one needs to engage with in order to sustain one's identity, or sense of self. Deprived of selfobjects, one is deprived of part of one's sense of self.

Lurie is arguably able to begin to reconcile himself to this self-dispossession because of a dawning recognition of the three truths about the indigenous Africans that produce compassion—namely, their suffering or need, their relative blamelessness, and their overlap with himself. The case can be made that he arrives at a tacit, not fully articulated grasp of these truths by recognizing their situatedness, their malleability, their heterogeneity, and his solidarity with them. In any case, the text provides evidence on the basis of which students operating with the four corrective general person-schemas that we have been discussing can arrive at these conclusions about the indigenous Africans.

Students can recognize Lurie's grasp of the rapists' situatedness and malleability in his response to Lucy's question, "Why did they hate me so? I had never set eyes on them." "It was history speaking through them," he replies. "A history of wrong. Think of it that way, if it helps. It may have seemed personal, but it wasn't. It came down from the ancestors" (156). Asked to explain what Lurie means by history here, students can observe that he is referring to the theft and destruction of the Africans' land, lifestyle, and lives by Lucy and Lurie's forbears. Teachers can then help the students explain how this history can be seen to speak through the rape. First, the history is responsible for a substantial portion of the rapists' present situation: the unequal distribution of wealth, property, and opportunities between indigenous Africans and Africans of European descent, a situation that is undoubtedly a causal factor in the perpetration of rape against a white person who has land by black persons who have not. And second, this history has operated powerfully on the rapists' formation, playing a major role in the development of their character, by forcing them, and the ancestors who passed down attitudes and values to them, to grow up in an apartheid society that inevitably fomented in them a justifiable anger, hatred, and resentment toward the European interlopers. Understanding the rapists in this way, as puppets of history, teachers can further explain, at least partly absolves them of blame for the attack.

Students should also be able to locate textual evidence that Lurie also recognizes that the rapists are in some important ways very much like him, or perhaps that he is very much like them. When his conversation with Lucy ends, he thinks about the three men and realizes that "he can, if he concentrates, if he loses himself, be there, be the men, inhabit them, fill them with the ghost of himself" (160). The recognition that indigenous Africans are at bottom not so different from Euro-Africans also comes to Lurie when he is thinking about Petrus, whom he suspects of complicity in the attack and whom he believes has designs on Lucy's land. Despite these reservations,

> he feels at home with Petrus, is even prepared, however guardedly, to like him.... What appeals to him in Petrus is his face and his hands. If there is such a thing as honest toil, then Petrus bears its marks. A man of patience, energy, resilience. A peasant, a *paysan*, a man of the country. A plotter and a schemer and no doubt a liar too, like peasants everywhere. Honest toil and honest cunning. (117)

Lurie's feeling of solidarity with Petrus is facilitated here by his recognition of Petrus's heterogeneity, the fact that, like people everywhere, he possesses both virtues and vices.

On the basis of this textual evidence, students should find it plausible that it is his recognition of the indigenous Africans' situatedness, malleability, heterogeneity, and solidarity that enables Lurie, despite his strong misgivings, to acquiesce in Lucy's plan to remain on her smallholding and offer her land and her hand to Petrus in exchange for his protection.

And it is in discussing and contemplating—and thus imaginatively rehearsing—Lucy's action script that Lurie comes to formulate a self-dispossession action script of his own. Teachers can help students develop metacognition of this process by pointing out to them that in discussing, contemplating, and writing about Lucy's action script—and also Lurie's—they themselves are enacting the same process by which Lurie comes to formulate his own self-dispossession action script.

Through his discussions with Lucy, Lurie gradually comes to accept and even admire her determination "to be a good mother" to the child of her rape and also a good person (216) and her resolution "to do anything, make any sacrifice, for the sake of peace" (208), "to start at ground level. With nothing.... No card, no weapons, no property, no rights, no dignity..., like a dog" (205). Lucy has come to realize that peace and justice require substantial self-dispossession on the part of her people, and Lurie realizes that her act of self-dispossession entails his own self-dispossession as well. He begins to relinquish his identity as a lover and a father and to contemplate becoming a grandfather and, ultimately, virtually nothing. Whereas he had earlier wept, in the passage quoted above, at the thought that his line would expire with Lucy's rape-child (199), now he contemplates this future with equanimity:

> So: once she was only a little tadpole in her mother's body, and now here she is, solid in her existence, more solid than he has ever been. With luck

> she will last a long time, long beyond him. When he is dead she will, with luck, still be here doing her ordinary tasks among the flowerbeds. And from within her will have issued another existence, that with luck will be just as solid, just as long-lasting. So it will go on, a line of existences in which his share, his gift, will grow inexorably less and less, till it may as well be forgotten. (217)

What Lurie occurs here, teachers can explain, is that Lucy's self-dispossession, and Lurie's as well, is compensated for and countered by being scripted in terms of generativity, which, as we discussed in Chapter 4, is the most fulfilling life script to which one can aspire. Insofar as one's solidarity extends to the others for whom one sacrifices oneself, one experiences in self-dispossession an extension of one's self rather than its diminution.

Charting the next steps of Lurie's progress should prove a bit easier for students. Through witnessing and sharing in Lucy's script of self-dispossession, Lurie is able to begin to enact his own self-dispossession. He is no longer opposed to changing. Though he will not be a lover or really a father any more, he is open to becoming a grandfather, thinking that as his passion wanes, he may develop other qualities, such as equanimity, kindliness, and patience, that will compensate for his loss of passion—a key component of his old identity—and serve as components of a new identity (217–218). He has a new start with Lucy, based on visitorship (218), and he has learned from Bev Shaw to love the dogs that he helps her euthanize. As the novel ends, Lurie carries Driepoot, the lame dog who loves him unconditionally and whom he has grown to love, "like a lamb" into the surgery to be euthanized. "'I thought you would save him for another week,' says Bev Shaw. 'Are you giving him up?' 'Yes, I am giving him up'" (220).

This is a richly symbolic, polysemous, and overdetermined ending, and its meaning is anything but univocal and obvious. But teachers can help their students see it as a kind of culmination of Lurie's self-dispossession and thus a possible model for their own self-dispossession action scripts. Lurie's euthanizing of his beloved dog is both generous to the dog, whose foreordained demise he helps make less lonely, traumatic, and painful, and an act of self-dispossession, insofar as the beloved dog is a selfobject, an integral part of Lurie's self. Moreover, the fact that Lurie carries Driepoot "like a lamb," evokes the Lamb of God and the Christian crucifixion, as well as, perhaps, Abraham's sacrifice of the ram as a stand-in for his son Isaac, both of which involve self-dispossession of what is most dear to the sacrificer in service to something the sacrificer recognizes as greater than himself. The novel's ending can thus be read as the ultimate act of self-dispossessing generosity, and Lurie may thus be seen to have enacted a script of profound self-dispossession at the end.

His various acts of self-dispossession—relinquishing his identities as a professor, lover, and father as well as selfobjects such as his home, his dog, his daughter (to a degree), and his culture (Beethoven, Janacek, the poets he loves)—can also function as a prototype, an action script, for the larger, collective self-dispossession of their cherished beliefs, values, cultural artifacts, way of life, and modes of enjoyment—in short, everything that makes them who they are—by Westerners, who must, if justice is to be served, or even if the apparent demographic inevitabilities play themselves out, ultimately cede dominance in all these areas to their various Others, many of whose identities, values, beliefs, behaviors, and lifestyles may be as antithetical to them as those of the rapists are to Lurie.

It will not be quick or easy for Western students to formulate action scripts of their own self-dispossession in this regard. But teachers can initiate the process, after leading them through the steps by which Lurie comes to his self-dispossession, by asking them to reflect and write about one of these Others, emulating Lurie's process as they do so. This will involve, first, registering and vividly imagining the relative deprivation—much of it severe—of the billions of people on the planet who do not live in the Western nations. It will also involve registering their differences from "us," and understanding those differences as products of their different current situations and their different formative environments. It will involve perceiving the common humanity (and perhaps also other types of overlap) that they share with us beneath the differences. And it will involve recognizing the responsibility that we Westerners bear for the plight of the deprived billions. Then, holding these truths about them firmly in mind, and experiencing the compassion for them—and the guilt—that will likely follow, students may be asked to develop, through reflection, discussion, and writing, an action script of their own for addressing the needs of this Other.

In engaging students in developing such action scripts, and in pursuing the other elements of cosmopolitan pedagogy put forth in this book, teachers might take Daru's treatment of his prisoner as a model. Like Daru, cosmopolitan educators hope their charges will free themselves from their ethnocentrism and engage with the larger world. And like

Daru, we try to provide them with enough provisions to sustain them on their journey—most notably in the present case, the provision of more adequate cognitive schemas and metacognition. But we must realize that some, and perhaps many, of our students will choose instead to remain captive, moving, if at all, only to a new locus of captivation: the world as a whole and/or the cosmopolitan approach to it will be too threatening for them to embrace. Like Daru, we cannot dictate which path they should follow. The best we can do, after providing our students with cosmopolitan cognitive capabilities, is to help them to develop metacognition about their own thinking and feeling concerning their options and to consider which path, ethnocentrism or cosmopolitanism, feels more like freedom and which feels more like captivity. Those who have become meta-cognizant of their generativity impulses, as discussed in Chapter 4, as well as their compassion and guilt, will be likely to experience cosmopolitanism as the path of freedom and fulfillment and will then proceed to formulate and enact specific, concrete action scripts for pursuing this path.

Notes

1 For an account of how people develop action scripts, see Huesmann.
2 On the establishment of action scripts through imaginative rehearsal, see Huesmann.
3 For a discussion of how much otherness a person can abide, see Palumbo-Liu.

Works Cited

Achebe, Chinua. "Africa's Tarnished Image." In *Things Fall Apart*. Ed. Francis Abiola Irele. New York: Norton, 2009. 209–220.

Achebe, Chinua. "An Image of Africa." In *The Norton Anthology of Theory and Criticism*. Ed. Vincent B. Leitch. New York: Norton, 2001. 1783–1794.

Achebe, Chinua. "Interview with Chinua Achebe." In *Things Fall Apart*. Ed. Francis Abiola Irele. New York: Norton, 2009. 121–135.

▶ Achebe, Chinua. "Teaching *Things Fall Apart*." In *Approaches to Teaching Achebe's* Things Fall Apart. Ed. Bernth Lindfors. New York: Modern Language Association, 1991. 20–24.

Achebe, Chinua. *Things Fall Apart*. New York: Anchor, 1994.

Alcorn, Marshall. *The Desire Not to Know*. New York: Palgrave Macmillan, 2013.

Allport, Gordon W. *The Nature of Prejudice*. New York: Addison-Wesley, 1979.

Anderson, Amanda. "Cosmopolitanism, Universalism, and the Divided Legacies." In *Cosmopolitics: Thinking and Feeling beyond the Nation*. Ed. Pheng Cheah and Bruce Robbins. Minneapolis: University of Minnesota P, 1998. 265–289.

Appiah, Kwame Anthony. *Cosmopolitanism: Ethics in a World of Strangers*. New York: Norton, 2006.

Atran, Scott. *In Gods We Trust: The Evolutionary Landscape of Religion*. New York: Oxford UP, 2002.

Attridge, Derek. *The Singularity of Literature*. New York: Routledge, 2004.
Avalos, Hector. *Fighting Words: The Origins of Religious Violence*. Amherst, NY: Prometheus, 2005.
Barrett, Justin. *Why Would Anyone Believe in God?* New York: Altamira P, 2004.
Beck, Ulrich. "The Cosmopolitan Society and Its Enemies." *Theory, Culture & Society* 19, 1–2 (2002): 17–44.
Bracher, Mark. "How to Teach for Social Justice: Lessons from *Uncle Tom's Cabin* and Cognitive Science." *College English* (March 2009):
Bracher, Mark. *Literature and Social Justice: Protest Novels, Cognitive Politics, and Schema Criticism*. Austin: University of Texas P, 2013.
Bracher, Mark. *Radical Pedagogy: Identity, Generativity, and Social Transformation*. New York: Palgrave Macmillan, 2006.
Bracher, Mark. "Schema Criticism: Literature, Cognitive Science, and Social Justice." *College Literature* 39 (Fall 2012): 84–117.
Bracher, Mark. *Social Symptoms of Identity Needs: Why We Have Failed to Solve Our Social Problems, and What to Do About It*. London: Karnac, 2009.
Brown, Garrett Wallace and David Held, eds. *The Cosmopolitanism Reader*. Malden, MA: Polity P, 2010.
Camus, Albert. "The Guest." Trans. Justin O'Brien. In *The Norton Anthology of World Literature*. Shorter 3rd edn. Ed. Martin Puchner, et al. Vol. 2. New York: Norton, 2013. 1512–1520.
Cheah, Pheng. "Cosmopolitanism." *Theory, Culture, & Society* 23(2006): 486–496.
Cialdini, Robert B., Stephanie L. Brown, Brian P. Lewis, Carol Luce, and Steven L. Neuberg. "Reinterpreting the Empathy-Altruism Relationship: When One into One Equals Oneness." *Journal of Personality and Social Psychology* 73.3 (1997): 481–494.
Clore, Gerald L., Karen Gasper, and Erika Garvin. "Affect as Information." In *Affect and Social Cognition*. Ed. Joseph P. Forgas. Mahwah, NJ: Erlbaum, 2001. 121–144.
Coetzee, J. M. *Disgrace*. New York: Penguin, 1999.
Cook, Guy. *Discourse and Literature*. New York: Oxford UP, 1995.
Cooper, Joel. *Cognitive Dissonance: Fifty Years of a Classic Theory*. Thousand Oaks, CA: Sage, 2007.
Costello, Kimberly and Gordon Hodson. "Exploring the Roots of Dehumanization: The Role of Animal-Human Similarity in

Promoting Immigrant Humanization." *Group Processes & Intergroup Relations* 13 (2009): 3–22.

Davis, Mark H., Laura Conklin, Amy Smith, and Carol Luce. "Perspective Taking on the Cognitive Representation of Persons: A Merging of Self and Other." *Journal of Personality and Social Psychology* 70.4 (1996): 713–726.

Dawkins, Richard. *The God Delusion*. New York: Houghton Mifflin Harcourt, 2006.

Dennett, Daniel C. *Breaking the Spell: Religion as a Natural Phenomenon*. New York: Penguin, 2006.

Diamond, Jared. *Guns, Germs, and Steel: The Fates of Human Societies*. New York: Norton, 1997.

Donald, James. "Internationalisation, Diversity and the Humanities Curriculum: Cosmopolitanism and Multiculturalism Revisited." *Journal of Philosophy of Education* 41.3 (2007): 289–308.

Eagleton, Terry. *The Idea of Culture*. Malden, MA: Wiley Blackwell, 2000.

Erikson, Erik. *Insight and Responsibility*. New York: Norton, 1964.

Galinsky, Adam D., Gillian Ku, and Cynthia S. Wang. "Perspective-Taking and Self-Other Overlap: Fostering Social Bonds and Facilitating Coordination." *Group Processes & Intergroup Relations* 8.2 (2005): 109–124.

Garbarino, James. *Lost Boys*. Free P, 1999.

Gaunt, Ruth. "Superordinate Categorization as a Moderator of Mutual Infrahumanization." *Group Processes & Intergroup Relations* 12 (2009): 731–746.

Gilligan, James. *Violence: Reflections on a National Epidemic*. New York: Vintage, 1997.

Griffith, Lucy F. "Combining Schema-Focused Cognitive and Psychodrama: A Model for Treating Clients with Personality Disorders." *Journal of Group Psychotherapy, Psychodrama, and Sociometry* 55 (2003): 128–140.

Harris, Sam. *The End of Faith: Religion, Terror, and the Future of Reason*. New York: Knopf, 2004.

Harris, Sam. *Letter to a Christian Nation*. New York: Knopf, 2006.

Haslam, Nick. "Dehumanization: An Integrative Review." *Personality and Social Psychology Review* 10 (2006): 252–264.

Heater, Derek. *World Citizenship: Cosmopolitan Thinking and Its Opponents*. New York: Continuum, 2002.

Works Cited

Held, David. *Cosmopolitanism: Ideals and Realities*. Malden, MA: Polity P, 2010.

Hitchens, Christopher. *God Is Not Great: How Religion Poisons Everything*. New York: Twelve, 2007.

Hitchens, Christopher, ed. *The Portable Atheist: Essential Readings for the Nonbeliever*. Philadelphia: Da Capo P, 2007.

Hogan, Patrick Colm. *The Culture of Conformism*. Durham, NC: Duke UP, 2001.

Hogan, Patrick Colm. "Literary Universals." In *Introduction to Cognitive Cultural Studies*. Ed. Lisa Zunshine. Baltimore: Johns Hopkins UP, 2010. 37–60.

Hollinger, David A. "Not Universalists, Not Pluralists: The New Cosmopolitans Find Their Own Way." In *Conceiving Cosmopolitanism: Theory, Context, and Practice*. Ed. Steven Vertovec and Robin Cohen. New York: Oxford UP, 2002. 227–239.

Huesmann, L. Rowell. "The Role of Social Information Processing and Cognitive Schema in the Acquisition and Maintenance of Habitual Aggressive Behavior." *Human Aggression: Theories, Research, and Implications for Social Policy*. Ed. Russell G. Geen and Edward Donnenstein. San Diego: Academic P, 1998. 73–109.

Iacoboni, Marco. *Mirroring People: The Science of Empathy and How We Connect with Others*. New York: Picador, 2009.

Jackman, M. R. and M. Crane. "'Some of My Best Friends Are Black'...: Interracial Friendship and Whites' Racial Attitudes." *Public Opinion Quarterly* 50: 459–486.

Jones, James M. *Prejudice and Racism*. 2nd edn. New York: McGraw-Hill, 1997.

Juergensmeyer, Mark. *Terror in the Mind of God: The Global Rise of Religious Violence*. Berkeley: University of California P, 2000.

Keen, Suzanne. *Empathy and the Novel*. New York: Oxford UP, 2007.

Keen, Suzanne. "A Theory of Narrative Empathy." *Narrative* 14 (October 2006): 207–236.

Lazarus, Richard S. *Emotion and Adaptation*. New York: Oxford UP, 1994.

Lazarus, Richard S. and Bernice N. Lazarus. *Passion and Reason: Making Sense of Our Emotions*. New York: Oxford UP, 1994.

Lerner, Melvin J. *The Belief in a Just World: A Fundamental Delusion*. New York: Plenum P, 1980.

Lerner, Melvin J. "Two Forms of Belief in a Just World." In *Responses to Victimizations and Belief in a Just World*. Ed. Leo Montada and Melvin J. Lerner. New York: Plenum P, 1998. 247–269.
Lessing, Doris. "The Old Chief Mshlanga." In *The Norton Anthology of Western Literature. Volume 2*. 8th edn. Ed. Sarah Lawall. New York: Norton, 2006. 2296–2304.
Levy, Sheri R., Antonio Freitas, and Peter Salovey. "Construing Action Abstractly and Blurring Social Distinctions: Implications for Perceiving Homogeneity Among, but Also Empathizing with and Helping Others." *Journal of Personality and Social Psychology* 83.5 (2002): 1224.
Lu, Catherine. "The One and Many Faces of Cosmopolitanism." *The Journal of Political Philosophy* 8.2 (2000): 244–267.
Maes, Jürgen. "Immanent Justice and Ultimate Justice: Two Ways of Believing in Justice." In *Responses to Victimizations and Belief in a Just World*. Ed. Leo Montada and Melvin J. Lerner. New York: Plenum P, 1998. 9–40.
Malcomson, Scott L. "The Varieties of Cosmopolitan Experience." In *Cosmopolitics: Thinking and Feeling beyond the Nation*. Ed. Pheng Cheah and Bruce Robbins. Minneapolis: University of Minnesota P, 1998. 233–245.
Miller, Dale T. "The Norm of Self-Interest." *American Psychologist* 54 (1999): 1053–1060.
Monroe, Kristen Renwick. *The Heart of Altruism: Perceptions of a Common Humanity*. Princeton: Princeton UP, 1996.
Montada, Leo and Melvin J. Lerner. "An Overview: Advances in Belief in a Just World Theory and Methods." In *Responses to Victimizations and Belief in a Just World*. Ed. Leo Montada and Melvin J. Lerner. New York: Plenum P, 1998. 1–7.
Montada, Leo and Melvin J. Lerner. "Preface." In *Responses to Victimizations and Belief in a Just World*. Ed. Leo Montada and Melvin J. Lerner. New York: Plenum P, 1998. vii-viii.
Moskowitz, Gordon B. "On Schemas and Cognitive Misers: Mental Representations as the Building Blocks of Impressions." *Social Cognition: Understanding Self and Others*. New York: Guilford, 2005. 153–192.
Nichols, Ashton. "The Politics of Point of View: Teaching *Things Fall Apart*." In *Approaches to Teaching Achebe's Things Fall Apart*. Ed. Bernth Lindfors. New York: Modern Language Association, 1991. 52–57.

Nussbaum, Martha C. *Cultivating Humanity: A Classical Defense of Reform in Liberal Education*. Cambridge, MA: Harvard UP, 1997.

Nussbaum, Martha C. "Patriotism and Cosmopolitanism." *For Love of Country: Debating the Limits of Patriotism*. Ed. Joshua Cohen. Boston: Beacon P, 1996. 2–17.

Nussbaum, Martha C. *Upheavals of Thought: The Intelligence of Emotions*. New York: Cambridge UP, 2001.

Oatley, Keith, Dacher Keltner, and Jennifer M. Jenkins. *Understanding Emotions*. 2nd edn. Malden, MA: Blackwell, 2006.

Padesky, Christine A. "Schema Change Processes in Cognitive Therapy." *Clinical Psychology and Psychotherapy* 1 (1994): 267–278.

Palumbo-Liu, David. *The Deliverance of Others: Reading Literature in a Global Age*. Durham: Duke UP, 2012.

Phillips, Stephen T. and Robert C. Ziller. "Toward a Theory and a Measure of the Nature of Nonprejudice." *Journal of Personality and Social Psychology* 72 (1997): 420–434.

Pinker, Steven. *The Blank Slate: The Modern Denial of Human Nature*. New York: Penguin, 2002.

Pyszczynski, Tom, Jeff Greenberg, and Sheldon Solomon. "A Dual-Process Model of Defense against Conscious and Unconscious Death-Related Thoughts: An Extension of Terror Management Theory." *Psychological Review* 106 (1999): 835–845.

Pyszczynski, Tom, Jeff Greenberg, and Sheldon Solomon. "Why Do We Need What We Need? A Terror Management Perspective on the Roots of Human Social Motivation." *Psychological Inquiry* 8 (1997): 1–20.

Robbins, Bruce. "Cosmopolitanism: New and Newer." *boundary 2* 34.3 (2007): 47–60.

Robbins, Bruce. "Introduction, Part I: Actually Existing Cosmopolitanisms." In *Cosmopolitics: Thinking and Feeling beyond the Nation*. Ed. Pheng Cheah and Bruce Robbins. Minneapolis: University of Minnesota P, 1998. 1–19.

Rorty, Richard. "Justice as a Larger Loyalty." In *The Rorty Reader*. Ed. Christopher J. Voparil and Richard J. Bernstein. New York: Wiley-Blackwell, 2010.

Ross, Lee and Richard E. Nisbett. *The Person and the Situation*. New York: McGraw-Hill, 1991.

Sachs, Jeffrey. *The End of Poverty: Economic Possibilities for Our Time*. New York: Penguin, 2006.

Schneider, David J. *The Psychology of Stereotyping*. New York: Guilford, 2004.

Schwartz, Regina M. *The Curse of Cain: The Violent Legacy of Monotheism*. Chicago: University of Chicago P, 1997.

Selengut, Charles. *Sacred Fury: Understanding Religious Violence*. New York: AltiMira P, 2003.

Sharot, Tali. *The Optimism Bias: A Tour of the Irrationally Positive Brain*. New York: Pantheon, 2011.

Sidanius, Jim and Felicia Pratto. *Social Dominance: An Intergroup Theory of Social Hierarchy and Oppression*. New York: Cambridge UP, 2001.

Singer, Peter. *The Life You Can Save: How to Do Your Part to End World Poverty*. New York: Random House, 2010.

Skrbis, Zlatko, Gavin Kendall, and Ian Woodward. "Locating Cosmopolitanism: Between Humanist Ideal and Grounded Social Category." *Theory, Culture & Society* 21.6 (2004): 115–136.

Smucker, Mervin R. and Jan Niederee. "Treating Incest-Related PTSD and Pathogenic Schemas Through Imaginal Exposure and Rescripting." *Cognitive and Behavioral Practice* 2 (1995): 63–93.

Solomon, Robert C. "In Defense of Sentimentality." In *Emotion and the Arts*. Ed. Mette Hjort and Sue Laver. New York: Oxford UP, 1997: 225–245.

Sookman Debbie and Gilbert Pinard. "Integrative Cognitive Therapy for Obsessive-Compulsive Disorder: A Focus on Multiple Schemas." *Cognitive and Behavioral Practice* 6 (1999): 351–362.

Stanton, Domna C. "Presidential Address 2005: On Rooted Cosmopolitanism." *PMLA* 121.3 (2006): 627–640.

Steinbeck, John. *The Grapes of Wrath*. Ed. Peter Lisca and Kevin Hearle. New York: Penguin, 1997.

Stevenson, Nick. "Cosmopolitanism and the Future of Democracy: Politics, Culture and the Self." *New Political Economy* 7.2 (2002): 251–267.

Stowe, Harriet Beecher. *Uncle Tom's Cabin*. 2nd edn. Ed. Elizabeth Ammons. New York: Norton, 2010.

Tan, Kok-Chor. *Justice without Borders: Cosmopolitanism, Nationalism and Patriotism*. New York: Cambridge UP, 2004.

Taylor, Charles. *The Ethics of Authenticity*. Cambridge, MA: Harvard UP, 1992.

Taylor, Shelley E. *The Tending Instinct: How Nurturing Is Essential to Who We Are and How We Live*. New York: Times, 2002.

Taylor, Shelley E. and Jennifer Crocker. "Schematic Bases of Social Information Processing." In *Social Cognition: The Ontario Symposium*. Ed. E. Tory Higgins, C. Peter Herman, and Mark P. Zanna. Hillsdale, NJ: Erlbaum, 1981. 89–134.

Todorov, Tzvetan. *Life in Common: An Essay in General Anthropology*. Trans. Katherine Golsan and Lucy Golsan. Lincoln, NB: U of Nebraska P, 2001.

Turner, Bryan S. "Cosmopolitan Virtue, Globalization and Patriotism." *Theory, Culture & Society* 19.1–2 (2002): 45–63.

Vertovec, Steven and Robin Cohen. "Introduction: Conceiving Cosmopolitanism." In *Conceiving Cosmopolitanism: Theory, Context, and Practice*. New York: Oxford UP, 2002. 1–22.

Vescio, Theresa K., Gretchen B. Sechrist, and Matthew P. Paolucci. "Perspective-taking and Prejudice Reduction: The Mediational Role of Empathy Arousal and Situational Attributions." *European Journal of Social Psychology* 33(2003): 455–472.

Voltaire. *Candide*. Trans. Lowell Bair. New York: Bantam, 1959.

Waldzus, Sven and Amélie Mummendey. "Inclusion in a Superordinate Category, In-Group Prototypicality, and Attitudes Towards Out-Groups." *Journal of Experimental Social Psychology* 40 (2004): 466–477.

Waldzus, Sven, Amélie Mummendey, and Michael Wenzel. "When 'Different' Means 'Worse': In-Group Prototypicality in Changing Intergroup Contexts." *Journal of Experimental Social Psychology* 41 (2005): 76–83.

Weiner, Bernard. *Judgments of Responsibility: A Foundation for a Theory of Social Conduct*. New York: Guilford P, 1995.

Wellman, James K., Jr., ed. *Belief and Bloodshed: Religious Violence across Time and Tradition*. Lanham, MD: Rowman & Littlefield, 2007.

Wells, Adrian. *Emotional Disorders and Metacognition*. New York: Wiley, 2000.

Young, Jeffrey D., Janet S. Klosko, and Marjorie E. Weishaar. *Schema Therapy: A Practitioner's Guide*. New York: Guilford P, 2003.

Zimbardo, Philip. *The Lucifer Effect: Understanding How Good People Turn Evil*. New York: Random House, 2007.

Zinn, Howard. *A People's History of the United States, 1492-Present*. Revised and Updated Edn. New York: HarperPerennial, 1995.

Index

Achebe, Chinua, 22–3, 26, 31, 36, 37, 39
  see also Things Fall Apart (Achebe)
action scripts, 19, 46–7, 106–28
activism, 4
Africans
  correcting faulty prototypes regarding, 20–3, 25–50
  Eurocentric schemas regarding, 54–62
  indigenous, 123–8
  prototypes regarding, 16–20
  sameness between Europeans and, 26, 38, 48–9
  stereotypes regarding, 12–13, 16–20, 29, 42–3, 45
agency, 15
Akunna (Things Fall Apart), 34–5
alienated labor, 88
Allport, Gordon, 63
altruism, 13, 86–92, 98
anger, 45–6
Appiah, Kwame, 4, 23n5
Arawak Indians, 71–2
Aristotle, 7
atomism, 98–100
attention, 11
autonomism, 100–5
Avalos, Hector, 85

beauty, standards of, 65

Belief in a Just World (BJW), 80–2
biases, 79–80
body images, 17, 36–7
brutality, 31, 60, 71–2
Bush, George W., 41, 78

Camus, Albert, 107–15
Candide (Voltaire), 63–92
  heterogeneity schema and, 97–8
  malleability schema in, 104
  optimism in, 66–73, 78
  prescription for happiness in, 86–92
  refutation of ontological ethnocentrism in, 77–86
  religious ethnocentrism in, 73–7
  situatedness schema in, 102–3
  social elitism and classism in, 64–6
  solidarity in, 99–100
capitalism, 88
caring, 89–90
Christianity, 34–5, 41–2, 47, 70, 74–5, 103
citizenship, 4–5
civic responsibility, 5–6
classical economics, 89
classism, 64–6, 92
Coetzee, J.M., 115–28
cognitive appraisal, 7–9

Index

cognitive dissonance, 52, 62–3, 122
cognitive distortions, 81
cognitive schemas, 11–15, 23n1, 52
  altering, via literary texts, 21–3
  changing faulty, 16–21
  correction of, 62–3
  ethnocentric, 54–62
  faulty, 53–4, 55–7
  harmful consequences of, 57–62
  regarding the Other, 54–5
cognitive science, 10–24
Cohen, Robin, 3
collective identity, 91–2
colonialism, 23n5, 71–2
Columbus, Christopher, 72
compassion, 5–9, 13, 45–6, 89, 107, 124
competition, 90
Conrad, Joseph, 36, 37
contentment, 87
Cook, Guy, 23n3
cooperation, 90
corrective exemplars, 113
cosmopolitan education, 2–3
cosmopolitanism
  action scripts for, 106–28
  behaviors constituting, 3–4, 16
  concept of, 1–9
  vs. ethnocentrism, 91–2
  as hospitality, 107–15
  promotion of, 2
  psychological factors in, 4–5
  as relinquishment of power, 115–28
Costello, Kimberly, 15
Crusades, 78
cultural openness, 4
customs, 38–9

David Lurie (*Disgrace*), 118–28
Dawkins, Richard, 85
death
  anxiety, 82–3
  beliefs about, 83–4
dehumanization, 12–15, 20, 26
Dennett, Daniel, 85
Diamond, Jared, 103
discrimination, 70–1

Disgrace (Coetzee), 106, 115–28
disposition, 4
dispositionism, 100–5
distributive justice, 4
District Commissioner (*Things Fall Apart*), 35, 42–3, 52–3
Donald, James, 3

education, cosmopolitan, 2–3
Ekwefi (*Things Fall Apart*), 32–3, 43
emotions, 6, 11
  prototypic, 18–19, 45–6
empathy, 4, 7–9, 95, 98
episode scripts, 17–18, 37–42
episodic memory, 11
Erikson, Erik, 88–9
essentialism, 100–5
ethnocentric cognitive schemas, 54–62
ethnocentric prototypes, correcting, 25–50
ethnocentric schemas
  in *Candide*, 63–92
  correction of, 62–3
  destructiveness of, 57–62
  ontological, 66–73
  in "The Old Chief Mshlanga," 53–63
ethnocentrism, 51, 52
  colonial, 71–2
  refutation of, 77–86
  religious, 73–7, 78–9
evolutionary psychology, 84–6
exemplars, 16, 21, 26, 27, 113
exploitation, 119–20
Ezinma (*Things Fall Apart*), 32, 43–4

false universals, 23n5
fear, 19
Freud, Sigmund, 80
fundamental attribution error, 8

generativity, 88–9
Gilligan, James, 31–2
global community, 5
global justice, 107, 116
The Grapes of Wrath (Steinbeck), 59

"The Guest" (Camus), 106, 107–15
guilt, 46

happiness, 87, 91
Harris, Sam, 85
Haslam, Nick, 14–15
Heart of Darkness (Conrad), 22, 28, 36, 37–8, 46
Heater, Derek, 2, 3, 4–5
helping behaviors, 3–4, 13, 16
Hess, Rudolph, 6
heterogeneity, 95–8, 111–12, 117, 124, 125
Hitchens, Christopher, 85
Hodson, Gordon, 15
homogeneity, 95–8
hospitality, 107–17
humanity
  vs. animality, 29–30
  shared, 13, 32, 127
human nature, 14–15, 94–105
human qualities, 14
human rights, 4
hypersensitive agency detection device (HADD), 84–5

identity, 15, 88, 90–2, 120
identity loss, 122, 123, 127
Ikemefuna (*Things Fall Apart*), 32
indigenous Africans, 123–8
indoctrination, 79
inferences, 11
information-processing scripts, 11, 16, 20–2, 48–9
infrahumanization, 12
in-groups, 12–13
intra-individual heterogeneity, 95–8, 111–12, 117

James, William, 6
judgments, 7–9, 11
  mistaken, 11–15
Juergensmeyer, Mark, 85
justice without borders, 6, 8

Keen, Suzanne, 7
Kendall, Gavin, 4

knowledge, types of, 11

Lerner, Melvin, 81, 82, 89
Lessing, Doris, 53–63
life scripts, 18, 42–4
literary imagination, 5, 6, 8–9
literary study
  to develop action scripts, 106–28
  to foster compassion and empathy, 5–9
  learning objectives for, 2–3
  to promote metacognition, 52–3
  as schema-altering apparatus, 21–3
literature, 5–7
Livingstone, David, 96
Lu, Catherine, 2

malleability, 100–11, 117, 124, 125
Marx, Karl, 80, 88, 98
metacognition, 20–2, 51
  of altruistic impulses, 86–92
  of death beliefs, 83–4
  defined, 52
  of ethnocentric schemas, 51–93
  ontological, 77–86
  promotion of, 52–3
  of psychological beliefs, 79–80
  and recognition of consequences, 57–62
  of religious beliefs, 73–9, 83–6
  of schema correction, 62–3
  of social elitism, 64–6
Miller, Dale T., 89
mirror neurons, 98
Modern Language Association (MLA), 2
Monroe, Kristen, 13
Montada,, 81
Mr. Brown (*Things Fall Apart*), 34–5, 41–2, 46–7
Mummendey, Amélie, 13

national citizenship, 5
nationalism, 69–71, 91, 92
Native Americans, 60, 61, 71–2
neurocognitive solidarity, 98

Nichols, Ashton, 49n1
Nussbaum, Martha, 5, 6, 7, 8–9

obligation, to help others, 3–5
Oedipus Rex, 44
Okonkwo (*Things Fall Apart*), 29–33, 37, 42, 43, 52–3, 103
"The Old Chief Mshlanga" (Lessing), 53–63
   ethnocentric schemas in, 54–62
   faulty schemas in, 55–7
   heterogeneity schema and, 97
   malleability schema in, 104
   schemas of the Other in, 54–5
   situatedness schema in, 102
   solidarity in, 99
ontological ethnocentrism, 66–73, 77–86
ontological solidarity, 98
openness, 4
oppression, 23–4n5
optimism, 66–73, 78
Other
   changing faulty person-schemas regarding, 16–21
   compassion for, 107
   correcting faulty prototypes regarding, 20–3, 25–50
   crucial truths about the, 95
   dehumanization of the, 14–15
   differences between self and, 101
   failure to recognize positive qualities in the, 26
   mistaken judgments concerning, 11–15
   perception of the, 113–15
   positive qualities of the, 117
   prototypes regarding, 16–20
   schemas about, 54–5
outgroups, 12–15

patriotism, 67
A People's History of the United States (Zinn), 72
person-schemas, 16–21, 94–105, 116–17
perspective taking, 8–9

Phillips, Stephen, 13–14
power, relinquishment of, 115–28
practical solidarity, 98
prejudice, 14
procedural memory, 11
productivity, 87–8
propositional knowledge, 11
propositions, 19–20
prototypes, 11, 12–20, 113
   correcting faulty, 20–3
   ethnocentric, correcting, 25–50
prototypic body images, 17, 36–7
prototypic emotions, 18–19, 45–6
prototypic individuals, 17, 28–35
psychological needs/biases, 79–80
Pyszczynski, Tom, 82–3

racism, 23n5
religion, 66–7, 69–72, 80, 83–6, 91
religious ethnocentrism, 73–9
rituals, 38–9
Rorty, Richard, 4

Sachs, Jeffrey, 115
schema-correcting techniques, 16–23
Schwartz, Regina, 85
Selengut, Charles, 85
self-dispossession, 115–16
self-interest, 89, 98
semantic memory, 11
shame, 32
shared humanity, 13, 32, 127
Singer, Peter, 114
situatedness, 100–5, 109–10, 117, 124, 125
Skrbis, Zlatko, 4
social cognition, 11
social elitism, 64–6
solidarity, 98–100, 112–13, 116–17, 124, 125
Solomon, Robert, 5
Stanton, Deborah, 2
Steinbeck, John, 59
stereotypes, 12–13, 16–20, 17, 95
   see also prototypes
Stevenson, Nick, 24n5

Stowe, Harriet Beecher, 9n2
strangers, compassion for, 5–9
suppositions, 11
sympathy, 6, 7

Taylor, Charles, 24n5
Taylor, Shelley, 89–90
Terror Management Theory (TMT), 82–3
Things Fall Apart (Achebe), 22–3, 25–50
   action scripts in, 46–7
   character descriptions in, 35–6
   corrective exemplars in, 26–7, 28–49
   ending of, 52
   episode scripts in, 37–42
   Europeans in, 34–5, 41–2
   goal of, 26
   heterogeneity schema and, 96–7
   information-processing routines in, 48–9
   life scripts in, 42–4
   malleability schema in, 103
   promotion of metacognition by, 52–3
   prototypes in, 27
   prototypic body images in, 36–7
   prototypic emotions in, 45–6
   prototypic individuals in, 28–35
   situatedness schema in, 101–2
   solidarity in, 99
   teaching of, 27–8, 47

Uchendu (*Things Fall Apart*), 33, 44

universalism, 23–4n5
universalist orientation, 13–14
Universalist Orientation Scale (UOS), 14
universal solidarity, 98–100
Unoka (*Things Fall Apart*), 32, 37, 44

Vertovec, Steven, 3
victims, blaming, 8, 81
violence, 31–2, 85
Voltaire, *Candide*, 63–92
voting, 4

Waldzus, Sven, 12–13
wealth redistribution, 116
Weiner, Bernard, 6
Wellman, James, 85
Wenzel, Michael, 13
Western brutality, 31
Westerners
   faulty prototypes regarding, 27, 34–5
   sameness between Africans and, 26, 38, 48–9
women, 119–23
Woodward, Bob, 41
Woodward, Ian, 4
work, 87–8
world citizenship, 4–5

Ziller, Robert, 13–14
Zinn, Howard, 72

GPSR Compliance
The European Union's (EU) General Product Safety Regulation (GPSR) is a set of rules that requires consumer products to be safe and our obligations to ensure this.

If you have any concerns about our products, you can contact us on

ProductSafety@springernature.com

In case Publisher is established outside the EU, the EU authorized representative is:

Springer Nature Customer Service Center GmbH
Europaplatz 3
69115 Heidelberg, Germany

www.ingramcontent.com/pod-product-compliance
Lightning Source LLC
LaVergne TN
LVHW041955060526
838200LV00002B/31